Curt Gasteyger
An Ambiguous Power

An Ambiguous Power

The European Union in a Changing World

Curt Gasteyger

Strategies for Europe

Bertelsmann Foundation Publishers
Gütersloh 1996

Die Deutsche Bibliothek – CIP-Einheitsaufnahme

Gasteyger, Curt:
An ambiguous power : the European Union in a changing world / Curt Gasteyger. –
Gütersloh : Bertelsmann Foundation Publ., 1996
(Strategies for Europe)
ISBN 3-89204-807-X

2. Auflage 1997
© 1996 Bertelsmann Foundation Publishers, Gütersloh
Vice president, politics division: Dirk Rumberg
Editor: Franco Algieri
Copy editor: Sabine Stadtfeld
Production editor: Sabine Klemm
Cover design: HTG Werbeagentur, Bielefeld
Cover photo: Geneviève Claisse, Paris, "Universaux", 1968
Typesetting: Utesch GmbH, Hamburg
Print: Fuldaer Verlagsanstalt GmbH
ISBN: 3-89204-807-X

4

Contents

Foreword

Europe is at a crucial stage of its development. It witnesses successful transformation processes in Eastern Europe, the association between the European Union and Central and East European countries as well as efforts to secure peace in former Yugoslavia. At the same time the integration process in Western Europe is proceeding and the enlargement of the European Union has become a dominant topic in the discussion on the future of Europe. All this is closely linked with the ambitious effort to establish a Common Foreign and Security Policy that is worth its name.

Against this background some major aspects have to be considered:
- It is not only necessary to ask whether or not the European Union and NATO will be extended to Central and East European countries, but also when this process will be completed and which countries will be members. Furthermore, it will be crucial how Russian politics develop. For the West European countries it has to be clear that a partnership with Russia is essential for the stability of the continent.
- Developing a comprehensive policy towards Eastern Europe should not lead to neglecting the Mediterranean region and weaken its importance for Europe. The European Union has laid the ground for an approach to the East and the South that forms the framework for stability and cooperation.
- To handle these challenging tasks will also mean to care for a balanced and strengthened transatlantic relationship. It would be

short-sighted to work on a new European architecture and on Europe's role in the world without considering the position of the United States.

The project 'Strategies for Europe' takes up such vital questions of European politics, trying to analyze them and to achieve a better understanding of Europe. In this context, Curt Gasteyger offers a valuable and critical contribution to the ongoing search for a European foreign and security policy identity. The author can draw on a long academic and practical experience in analyzing European developments and with this work he has set a point of reference to better understand Europe.

Prof. Dr. Dr. h.c. Werner Weidenfeld
Member of the Board of the
Bertelsmann Foundation
Director of the
Center for Applied Policy Research
at the Ludwig-Maximilians-University of Munich

Summary

Europe with, at its core the European Union, is today at a cross-roads: it will have to decide whether, at the end of this century, it will transform itself from a powerful economic community into an equally powerful political actor. In so doing it would assume the kind of responsibilities that correspond to its own potential and influence and that a difficult and disorderly world expects and no doubt needs.

Getting close to the age of forty, the European Union should be in its prime. It has been the central architect of West European recovery and German-French reconciliation. It has weathered successfully the challenge of the Cold War. Four times it has admitted new members growing from a small nucleus of six to a respectable group of fifteen. It moved from a 'Community' to a 'Union' – a highly ambitious term waiting to be translated into political reality.

Expectations about the place and role this Union should, and will, have to play in the world of tomorrow are therefore high indeed. But 'Europe', however defined, is not yet an entity in and of international politics. The Union's common foreign and security policy is still in its infancy. There is still a wide gap between what the Union can do – and in fact is doing – in the economic field and what it should do in those of foreign and security policy.

The potential is there but the political will is still all too often absent. Member states still want to guard what they consider their precious if not inalienable right of self-determination in the almost sacrosanct fields of foreign and security matters. Consensus building, let alone

11

majority vote therefore remain difficult. Sometimes it is even outright impossible.

And yet, the Union faces an international environment which requires common action. It has also, over the years, developed a whole range of instruments and policies by and with which it can pursue effectively its own interests and serve those of other regions and countries. There is a host of bilateral and multilateral agreements, mostly on trade, assistance and aid. They range from the Lomé Convention with some seventy developing countries via the Europe Agreements with now ten Central and East European countries, to agreements on partnership and cooperation with Russia, Ukraine and other members of the Commonwealth of Independent States (CIS). The Union is present in the G-7 and the Organization for Security and Cooperation in Europe (OSCE) meetings; it has signed a transatlantic declaration with the United States and Canada, and has established relationships of various kinds with regional organizations in the Middle East, South East Asia and Latin America.

In order to act more forcefully and effectively, the Union will have to choose from this global array of commitments and agreements a few which deserve priority. Three of them come to mind. They relate to the three peripheries of a wider Europe: Central and Eastern Europe, including Russia; the wider Balkans, including Turkey; and the Mediterranean, above all North Africa.

These three areas form the crucial core whose economic development and political consolidation will also determine that of the Union and of Europe as a whole.

From here a fourfold strategy should be developed. It should be aimed at,

- first, formulating a new *finalité politique* making the European Union the principal promoter and stabilizing factor of the wider Europe and the adjacent areas;
- second, rendering the Union's foreign and security policy more effective by reducing its scope and focussing it on the 'feasible essentials'; i.e. on those areas which demand common action and for which there is no substitute by way of individual action;
- third, opting, in the interest of preserving the greatest possible inter-

nal cohesion, either for a 'sectoral neutrality' on issues on which no consensus can be reached, or for allowing 'ad-hoc coalitions-for-actions' where, with the tacit agreement of all, only some member states are ready and capable to act;
– fourth, broaden the scope and direction of 'conditionality' by using still more purposefully the Union's unique economic potential for attaining political objectives of general importance.

Such proposals provide no panacea for making the Union a united and powerful international actor. But they are feasible within the existing institutional and legal framework. Above all they help to narrow down the gap between the Union's remarkable power potential and its still deplorable insufficiency when it comes to putting to use the former for the benefit of all. Thus, with the double challenge of external enlargement and internal reform, the European Union will have to prove that it can be respectful of the sensitivities and interests of its own members while becoming even more responsive to the needs and expectations of the world outside.

Geneva, October 1995

Introduction

Europe's ascendancy and decline, its mission and demise[1] were forecast many times. The forecasts for both often turned out to come true – but rarely in the way expected. Europeans have thus become cautious when asked to make yet another prediction as to their future role and place in the world of tomorrow. Since 1939 they have lived through the shattering experience of the Second World War, the humiliating frustration of the Cold War and, most recently, the disappointing and disquieting sequel of the period after. Having lost much of their global clout during and after the Second World War, and having lived for forty years in the shadow of two major powers – the United States and the Soviet Union – little confidence remains as to what political power this shattered continent should or could assume in the future.

Europe: victim and beneficiary of the Cold War

'Global reach' is no longer on the European agenda, let alone in the capacity of most European states. France and Britain are only partial exceptions. They have preserved some of their former political status and military muscle. They are permanent members of the UN Security Council. They possess nuclear weapons. And they entertain, either by

---

1   After the title of Denis de Rougemont's book, Mission ou démission de la Suisse, Neuchâtel 1940.

15

way of the 'Commonwealth' or the 'Communauté' a network of relations and affinities no other European country can boast of. And yet,
they too have lost much of their former power and glory. As they
withdrew from their colonial empires they became more specifically
European – the Netherlands in the Forties, France in the Fifties, Belgium in the Sixties, Portugal in the Seventies, and Britain over a period
of twenty years up to the end of the Sixties. It was by no means an easy
process. It required an adjustment to more limited, i.e. continental
proportions. This was easier for France. For reasons of her geographic
position, she had always been a continental power. In addition, she
could aspire for a leading position there if peace remained assured and
her arch-rival Germany controlled. The concept of European integration, as developed and initiated by Robert Schuman and Jean Monnet,
provided both. At the same time it gave France the necessary economic
backing for her international role in general, and in francophone Africa in particular. France, in other words, made up her loss of international status by becoming the leading promoter of European integration.

The case of Britain was different. Together with France she suffered
a humiliating defeat during the so-called Suez crisis in 1956. By confronting Egypt's vociferous and nationalistic president Nasser they
pursued similar though not fully congruent aims: France feared Nasser's influence on Algerian nationalists fighting for independence
against the French colonial 'métropole'; Britain in turn feared for her
control over the Suez canal – in her view the indispensable strategic
link between her outposts in the Mediterranean and her presence 'East
of Suez', stretching from the Gulf via Singapore up to the eastern most
outpost of Hong Kong. But both France and Britain, linked in an
'unholy alliance' with Israel, wanted the demise of Nasser. After a few
days of military action they had, however, to withdraw – and did so
under the combined pressure of the United States and the Soviet Union.
These two and not any longer Europe's traditional colonial powers
were now on the ascendance on the world stage. In different ways and
with different success they both were set to compete for the spoils of
the former French, British and, later, also Portuguese empires.

The bitter experience of 1956 accelerated British retreat from her colonial empire. Slowly and reluctantly London turned its eyes and interests towards the continent and to the nascent European Community. But Britain's rapprochement with continental West Europe was prompted more by economic than political considerations. When she eventually joined the Community in 1972 it was clear that she expected economic advantages in the first place rather than an accretion of political influence. Her vision of whether the Community should evolve into a political unit and how this would affect her own role in it, thus clearly differed from that of France.

When Spain and Portugal, two other former colonial powers, entered the Community ten years later, they had both left behind their global aspirations. To them the Community was a European institution offering substantial economic advantages but hardly a return to former extra-continental influence. For the latter they were compensated in an unexpected way. Both, to a different degree, were able – thanks to their membership with the Community – to develop a new profile in foreign policy. In a sense, the hitherto insurmountable barrier of the Pyrenees, was removed: they could become part and parcel of the process of 'Europeanized' policy making. No longer did they feel peripheral or isolated nor indeed were they treated as such by their fellow member countries. Almost overnight they had to define their foreign policy in a European context – with rewards not coming from distant overseas possessions but from Brussels. Work within the framework of European Political Cooperation (EPC), later the Common Foreign and Security Policy (CFSP), required a shift of priorities by making their national interests gradually more compatible with those of the Community.[2]

Germany and Italy, the two defeated Axis powers, had long given up their extra-European ambitions. They were constrained in what they could do in foreign policy though Italy maintained her links and affinities with the Mediterranean, Germany, now divided, kept alive her interest in Central and Eastern Europe. Her 'Ostpolitik' was, however, first and foremost a function of her desire to reunify with its now

2   Cf. Franco Algieri and Elfriede Regelsberger (eds.), Spain and Portugal in European Foreign Policy, Bonn 1996.

communist-ruled Eastern part. As such it was directed primarily at Moscow on whose policy and interests such reunification crucially depended.

All this was and is a far cry from Europe's erstwhile global presence and commitments. The European Community was not conceived as the springboard for a European global come-back. Its two principal and interlinked objectives were, first, the prevention of war via peaceful reconciliation, and second, economic recovery and progress via gradual integration. The confrontation with the Soviet-dominated East added soon a third dimension, that of resisting the latter's socio-ideological or military-political onslaught. Together these three objectives may be called inward-looking and defensive. They were surely not expansionist or offensive – as Communist propaganda then would have it, or as one might have expected from an economically ever more prospering group of six, nine and then twelve West European countries.

Still, the very concept that integration was possible between 'capitalist' states, went against deeply ingrained communist doctrine. Lenin, in his pamphlet *On the Slogan of the United States of Europe*, written in August 1915, polemicised against such an idea: according to him "the United States of Europe under capitalist conditions would be either impossible or reactionary"[3]. He feared both the attractiveness of such an 'integration' and a strengthening of the capitalist world as a consequence of it. This was precisely what his successors, from Stalin via Khrushchev to Brezhnev, feared as well when faced with the emerging European Community. To them, this community was an economic challenge as much as a threat to Soviet dominance on the continent. A strong and united Western Europe, with the Federal Republic as its Eastern-most spearhead, was seen as the economic basis of NATO and, as such, a counterweight if not outright challenge to the 'Eastern bloc'.

As the East-West climate gradually improved and 'peaceful coexistence' became the catchword of Soviet foreign policy, pragmatism began to prevail over dogmatism. Brezhnev, in his speech on March

---

3   Wladimir Illjitsch Lenin, Über die Losung der Vereinigten Staaten von Europa, Werke. Band 21 (August 1914 – December 1915), Berlin 1960, pp. 342–346.

20th, 1972, declared his country's willingness to cooperate with the Community. It was the beginning of a modus vivendi between the two economic organizations.[4] But it took another fifteen years before a breakthrough in the relationship between the Community and the Council on Mutual Economic Assistance (COMECON) became possible. Shortly before the collapse of the Eastern bloc, in June 1988, an agreement was signed between the two organizations – the European Commission representing the Community – stipulating the establishment of official relations. To little avail: the Community did not need Soviet recognition to prove that it had already been for a long time an international actor in its own right; for the COMECON the recognition came too late: like the Warsaw Pact it decided its own dissolution only three years after this agreement, in June 1991.

In what used to be called the 'Third World', the Community and later the European Union was seen in a quite different light. Many, if not most developing nations expected economic and financial aid from it. To them, the Community appeared not only rich economically but also acceptable politically. With no imperial ambitions and no capacity for global strategic reach anymore, it presented a less imposing and more promising alternative to the two superpowers always suspected of more sinister intentions.[5] While being directly and actively involved in the East-West contest, it was seen, not unlike the Third World, as being also a target of this contest as well as a stage on which this contest was being fought out.

The European Community was thus both beneficiary and a victim of the Cold War. The latter had no doubt an integrating effect on the Community. The idea of a 'common and present danger' facilitated consensus and compromise amongst the member states. It generated feelings of political homogeneity or at least solidarity, of a kind which a Europe undivided and without the looming fear of nuclear confrontation had never known so far. As *détente* slowly replaced sterile con-

---

4   Christoph Royen and Eberhard Schulz, Wandel in Osteuropa, in: Eberhard Schulz (ed.), Die Ostbeziehungen der Europäischen Gemeinschaft, Munich 1977, pp. 146 ss.
5   Cf. Max Kohnstamm and Wolfgang Hager (eds.), Zivilmacht Europa – Supermacht oder Partner, Frankfurt 1973 (English version: A Nation Writ Large ? Foreign Policy Problems before the European Community, London 1973).

frontation, rifts and differences re-appeared amongst the members when it came to formulate a common policy vis-à-vis the East in general and the Soviet Union in particular.[6] As was said towards the end of the Cold War: "Opinions (in the West in general, and in Western Europe in particular) vary widely as to the means and the methods by which a change in the status quo in Europe should be brought about. [...] Reaching a consensus in the West that goes beyond paying lip-service to the ideal of a 'free' or more 'humane' Eastern Europe, is a constant challenge. It is not at all clear that, forty years after World War II, West Europeans have enough good reasons to induce them to go through the tedious process of building a consensus around a policy whose merits and impact they doubt".[7]

With hindsight it became clear that there was rarely, if ever, a common policy of the Community vis-à-vis the 'Communist bloc' beyond the will for common defence and some very general statements about common goals. It is important to remember this for two reasons: first, because it shows that even under the conditions of the Cold War the Community seldom succeeded in developing – and sustaining – a common position in the field of foreign policy. It can be – rightly – argued that this lay neither in its competence nor that it was indispensable. Still, it is interesting to note that under conditions of a commonly perceived threat and in the shadow of a military superpower with hegemonic aspirations, the Community was extremely reluctant to push for more than very lofty declarations on central foreign policy issues.

In search of 'identity'

And yet it was called upon several times to do so. The Cold War was, however stable it appears now to many in hindsight, far from being a period of general international tranquility. While it was relatively easy

---

6   Cf. the study on Soviet – East European Relations as a Problem for the West; ed. by Richard D. Vine, Beckenham/Kent 1987.
7   Curt Gasteyger, Conclusions: Western Interests, Policy, Dilemmas and Prospects, in: R. Vine, op. cit., p. 247.

for the Community to 'speak with one voice' when it came to condemning aggressive acts of Soviet policy or standing up to challenges of communist ideology, it was much more difficult, or delicate, to do so on issues outside the East-West conflict. Fortunately, there were, in the 1960s and 1970s, rather few such issues on which the Community felt obliged to express a common view. The recurring instance was the conflict in the Middle East, in particular the two Arab-Israeli wars in 1967 and 1973, respectively, the latter prompting also an oil embargo on part of the OPEC states against the West. Here, the Community was directly affected in its economic interests. It thus could not but take a firm and united stand. It did so reluctantly and not very convincingly. Perceptions and interests of its members with regard to Israel on the one hand, the Arab states on the other, diverged while at the same time practically all member countries depended more or less on Gulf and North African oil. In other words: "The October war (of 1973) and the energy crisis have made it inevitable and imperative for the European Community to get involved in the Middle East, economically and politically".[8] In a sense, then, this was the first time when the Community had to formulate a common position on a foreign policy issue outside the Cold War context. It may have done so rather meekly at its Copenhagen summit meeting in December 1973. But at least it did it. In a rather solemn document on 'European identity' the nine member states acknowledged their global responsibility and pledged to play an 'active role in world politics'. They thus sent out a signal to both the United States and to the Middle East saying that the Community would henceforth 'collaborate in the establishment and maintenance of peace, stability and progress in this region' – a pledge which the European Union still upholds though with rather modest results.

An explanation for this may be found in the fact that much of what constituted the strategic dimension of East-West relations was left to the United States and the Soviet Union. In this sense Europe in general, the European Community in particular, was a victim of the East-West confrontation. Both Eastern and Western Europe were drawn in, and

---

8   Karl Kaiser, The Energy Problem and Alliance Systems: Europe, The Middle East and the International System. Adelphi Papers 115 (Spring 1975), p. 23.

became part of, this overarching rivalry. Together they found themselves locked into a seemingly endless confrontation between irreconcilable socio-political systems. On a global level, ever more issues were seen and handled as if they were part and parcel of this confrontation. It seemed almost impossible to act independently. Nobody wanted to be suspected of betrayal to the good cause of one or the other side. Infinite energies were thus spent, first, in the attempt to prevail in, and then in the search for mutual accommodation to, this confrontation.

Such energies, both political and economic, could have been spent more fruitfully for better purposes. The Cold War induced the Europeans to focus their attention too much, if not sometimes too exclusively, on themselves. For Western Europe this had at least the advantage of promoting integration. It had, on the other hand, the negative effect of lowering Europe's profile in the world and of making it an accomplice of superpower hegemonic aspiration. It was therefore hardly an incentive to formulate common positions of one's own. In short, the Community's attitude towards major international issues and in particular towards the communist East lived very much from strength borrowed from the United States.

On the lower, operational or tactical level, particularly the policies of the member states rarely coalesced into strong common positions. Within the overall framework of the East-West battle there did not seem to be a need for a specific European position. As a consequence, governments were reluctant to expose themselves to the rarely edifying exercise of searching for common positions on what seemed secondary issues. Under such favourable or better perhaps, unfavourable circumstances their was little need to develop the habit of joint policy making let alone creating the instruments that made it work.

Those who criticize the absence of an effective foreign and security policy of the European Union should keep these circumstances in mind. One can, and possibly even should, deplore such a glaring gap between potential and performance. Its negative effect on the Union's internal cohesion and external presence is being felt even more acutely now that the rigidities of the Cold War are being replaced by uncertainties of an ever more fragmented and conflict-prone continent. But it should not be forgotten that, as Soviet-American competition acquired global and ever more military dimensions, the European Community gained in stature and attractiveness. As mentioned before, it was appreciated, if not admired, by the non-aligned world precisely because it was *not* a superpower. Europe's weakness on a global scale became in a way its strength, and its prospering economy ever more an asset.

Paradoxically, the end of the Cold War did not undermine this high opinion of the Community. Quite the contrary. There was first the demise of the Soviet Union and the political-economic model it had tried to sell to, or even impose on, its allies and friends around the globe. Soviet military power or 'global reach' turned out to be based on a very thin and fragile economic base. Having been overstretched for years, it broke at the same time as its own promoter, Moscow. As the Soviet Union and its main successor, the Russian Federation, withdrew from the world scene, it became clear that henceforth economic and technological rather than military power would be the determining factor of international relations.

The United States, the only remaining superpower, got this message as well. It, too, had come close to overstretch. It, too, had to streamline and reduce its strategic commitments. And it, too, recognized that its new and no less serious competitors were no longer in the military but in the non-military field; economic performance, technological innovation, instant communication and financial mobility became the catchwords of a newly emerging post-Cold War world. And the competitors were no longer Russia but Japan, South-East Asia, even the former enemy China and, last but not least, the European Community.

Between aspiration and reality

Indeed, the change of parameters and the shift from military power to economic competition have put the Community into an entirely different category of players. Almost all of a sudden its weakness or its 'incompleteness' as a military power became less embarrassing and conspicuous and its real strength – economic integration and performance – moved to the front stage. In other words: the environment in which we will have to define Europe's future role, its place and its interests in the world, has profoundly changed. To be sure, it may change again. Military power still remains a, if not the central element of international security. But with the break-up of the Soviet Union, with German unification and a full or partial withdrawal of Soviet and American forces, respectively, Europe has regained a freedom of action it had not enjoyed since the end of World War II. The real revolution in Europe in these turbulent years after 1989 is that Europe and the Europeans have become again masters of their own political destiny.[9] From this follows that it will be responsible again not only for the political order on the continent but also for the way its weight and interests influence the wider world. While the former relates to internal European matters and can therefore be relatively easily defined, the latter immediately raises a host of questions.

The first question is the inevitable one of what is meant by 'Europe'. It is probably as old as Europe itself. In our context it is relevant only insofar as it relates to the extent to which the 'core' of Europe, the European Union, can and should take on new members and, if so, which ones. Europe's postwar division has taught us to think in terms of a 'small Europe' – a Europe reduced both in its political status and its geographic size. It came very close to Paul Valéry's description of Europe as the appendix to the Eurasian landmass. 'Small' was not only beautiful but, in terms of assuming international responsibility, it was convenient. This was true, on a national level, also for Germany. The price for both, Europe and Germany was division, the 'protective presence of the super-powers' and, last but not least, the apparent permanent loss of Central and Eastern Europe. When talking of Europe few, if any thought of this lost part of the continent, stretching from the Baltic Sea via Czechoslo-vakia southwards to the Balkans. These countries and regions were, in the minds of many, 'written off', lost for an indefinite future to the unyielding hegemony of an ever powerful Soviet Union.

---

9   The only important exception though being the Soviet-American system of nuclear deterrence on which European security depended in such a literally vital way. Whether this system is still a reality in view of the breakdown of the Soviet Union, is one question, whether it is still important for European security, is another. The answer to both would seem to be, at least for the time being, a 'no'.

With the division of Germany, Europe had also lost its traditional geographic centre. It had shifted westwards. It made France the political and Brussels the institutional pillar of this Western centred and American oriented semi-continent. The non-members of the gradually expanding European Community, the neutral and non-aligned countries of various size and status, surrounded this new core. They basically shared its political, economic and cultural values and outlooks. They profited from its political stability. And they did not mind in the least that this Europe did not or was unwilling to play a global role.

This Europe was content with itself. To be sure, it was lopsided in many ways. Above all, it was truncated and incomplete. While prospering economically, it had some difficulty in defining its political identity. The experience when faced with the October war in the Middle East and the ensuing oil embargo, referred to above, showed how difficult it was to define such a political identity. It was a *prise de conscience* undertaken not out of its own volition but in face of an unexpected and serious external challenge. The Copenhagen declaration of December 1973 turned out to be a rather difficult exercise when Community members had to define not only what they were all against but what objectives they were prepared to pursue together. It forced the Nine to state publicly their global obligations that they were called upon to assume as the price and reward of their unification.

What matters here is not so much how the 'European identity' was eventually understood and defined. This is, and will remain, an interesting question under any circumstances. What matters in this specific context is the link that the Nine made for the first time between their efforts at unification and the global responsibilities they recognized should follow from it. From then on, this link was officially and publicly established. Without a serious loss of credibility it could not be severed again. One is the function of the other. Or, to put it differently: the degree of unification in the sense of both 'deepening' and 'enlarging' determines also the scope and direction of the Community's global reach and responsibilites. Optimists may go even one step further and turn this relationship around: the more the European Union is involved in global affairs, the greater the need for its acting in unison.

Reality so far has been different. 'Europe' – however defined – is not, or not yet, an entity in and of international politics. Even the European Union is rarely operationally effective and institutionally efficient when it has to act as a single entity. The pragmatic approach was preferred to too heavy an insistence on often artificial common positions. Member states were, and still are, allowed to exercise much freedom in the formulation of their foreign policy. By preferring a case-to-case consensus to long-term commitments they promote the de facto consolidation of such common policy. The sheer routine of daily and regular contacts between the foreign ministries creates habits and promotes understanding and thus prepares the ground for ever more concerted action. Still, a common foreign policy is not yet in sight even though the Maastricht Treaty has given it a modest institutionalized framework.

Vast differences if not divergencies nevertheless remain. It did not need the Gulf war – Iraq's occupation of Kuwait in early August 1990 – to prove it. When it comes to specifics and to common actions, Europe still falls far short of both its reputation as a highly industrialized and wealthy continent whose potential as a group of politically stable democracies should, in theory, enable it to yield considerable influence if not power. So far each country is still very much on its own when it comes to foreign policy. Each maintains its own profile and pursues its own interests. Each has its own *domaine réservé* of sorts. The latter may dwindle as the CFSP develops. But a nucleus of varying size and resilience is likely to survive. France will want to retain her manifold 'special relationships' with francophone countries; Britain takes it for granted to stay in the centre of the Commonwealth with all the commitments attached to it; Italy sees for herself a special role in the Mediterranean and has as yet an unresolved territorial dispute with Slovenia. Spain is proud of its good relations with Latin and Central America. And everybody is anxiously following the re-emergence of Germany's new-old connections with Central and Eastern Europe, including yet another *entente* with Russia.

All this is far from bad in itself. In most cases, it is the legacy of Europe's past and its wide-ranging interests in, and affinities with, the surrounding world. In using them properly and jointly Europe can, or could, establish a wider and denser network of relations than any other

26

power, the United States included, can boast of today. It spreads over nearly the entire globe. As such it could become a unique asset for making Europe's influence felt and serving its own interests.

Whether or not Europe can and should assume global responsibilities (to take up again the term of the Copenhagen declaration) will therefore not only depend on how Europe is defined. It will depend even more crucially on what kind of responsibilities Europe, the European Union, should assume, how they should be carried out and, last but not least, for what kind of purpose. In other words: we will have to think about, first, the priorities of a common foreign policy, i.e. its political dimension; second, about its scope, i.e. the geographic dimension; and, third, its *finalité*, i.e. its conceptual dimension or, more simply, the objectives it is expected to attain or the missions it will be called up to fulfill.

This means that it is not enough to expect Europe to have a foreign policy and to speak, as the saying goes, 'with one voice'. The more difficult question is rather what kind of policy it should be and how it should be pursued. Surely, it would have to be a policy that serves Europe's own and well understood interest. But, one might think, also a policy that contributes to the stabilization of Europe's periphery and, more ambitiously, to the shaping of a world order of which Europe wants to be a part.

Are these expectations realistic? The following chapters are a provisional and no doubt incomplete attempt at a tentative answer. We will look, first, at the profound restructuring the world is presently undergoing and ask whether and how it affects Europe's view of itself and its position in this newly emerging order. We will then look at the changing landscape in Europe itself with its many new and old fault-lines and its widening horizon. The third chapter will take a look at what might be called 'the instruments of power' whilst the fourth and fifth are devoted to new concerns and vulnerabilities. The former refers to the ways and means by which influence can be and is being exerted in an era in which economic power and technological know-how ever more overshadow political-military might; the latter refers to manifold challenges modern industrialized societies and Europe are being faced with. These five chapters should provide, it is hoped, the kind of background against which we may be able to identify some important centres of concern when the European Union will have to define and formulate its foreign policy interests and the ways and means by which these are, or should be, pursued. We should then be in a better position to judge the Union's potential of as well as the limits to its foreign policy making. In a concluding chapter we will try to see what Europe's position could or should be in the world of tomorrow. This will be at best an attempt to draw up an agenda for action, or more likely, simply a list of Europe's deficits in face of an ever more demanding and disorderly world.

I. The Changing International Environment

Europe, in the twentieth century, has lived through several revolutions. Perhaps the biggest was caused by the combined events that led to both its demise as a centre of world politics and to its partition into two politically and ideologically antagonistic blocs. There is probably no region in the world of similar size and importance that within such a short time span has undergone a more profound change of status, loss of power and degree of self-destruction than Europe. After the First World War and even more so after the Second, Europe became the very symbol and incarnation of Oswald Spengler's somber prediction of the 'decline of the Occident'.

A Cold War *avant la lettre*

The First World War, as unnecessary as bloody, was clearly the beginning of this decline. This war became not only the midwife of the Bolshevik revolution. It brought also the demise of the two central European empires, Germany and Austria. And it spelled the end of yet another empire, that of the Ottomans. Together, this process – euphemistically called 'self-determination' – split major parts of Central and Eastern Europe into many small, often antagonistic and economically hardly viable parts. Communist Russia remained the only multinational power of imperial size and ambition. It refused, however, to be part of a world that it considered to be doomed. It withdrew into its shell by building 'Socialism in one country' and leaving the world arena to whatever power, whether of colonial tradition or hegemonic ambition, still remained. To the former belonged Britain and France, to the latter expansionist Japan and, later on, nationalist Germany under Hitler's direction.

The institutional focus of world politics during the interwar period was the League of Nations. It was Europe-centred mainly because of the absence of the two powers which, a quarter of a century later, were to become the dominant players in a very different game, called the Cold War, i.e. the United States and the Soviet Union.

The period between the two world wars thus turned out to be an interlude, or, better perhaps, the gestation period of an emerging confrontation. Its roots can in fact be detected in the two opposing concepts, first, of man's and society's future and following from that, the organization of international order. This clash not of civilizations but of ideas was personified in Woodrow Wilson and Wladimir Illjitsch Lenin and their vision of the future of mankind. The first wanted to revolutionize the international system, the second national societies. Both wanted to change the world, one from above, the other from below, either by insisting on national self-determination, collective security and new forms of international cooperation, or by spreading the gospel of a class- and stateless society with the promise of the final victory of communism and hence peace.

In concept, if not in reality, the world was already then heading for a division. The polarity of ideas and policies proclaimed and pursued by the leaders of America and Russia seemed foreordained. The stage was set for the clash between bourgeois democracy and proletarian dictatorship, between socialism and Soviet communism, the League of Nations and the Comintern, democracy versus totalitarianism or simply Wilson versus Lenin.[10]

It was, in a sense, a Cold War *avant la lettre*. It did not, in the interwar period, acquire global dimensions. Nor did it have, as its ultimate sanction, the threat of nuclear holocaust that became so dominant after the Second World War. The explanation for such postpone-

10 Dietrich Geyer, Die russische Revolution, Stuttgart 1968, p. 134.

ment would seem simple: neither power appeared as a major player on the global state. Rather they stayed in the wings. As regards the United States, President Wilson's hope for a leading role of his country in the League did not come to pass. It withdrew again into its shell of distant neutrality. In the now communist Russia priority was given first to a reconstitution of the empire and, then, to its internal reorganization and fortification. Lenin's heir, Stalin, decided to build 'socialism' at home before expanding it abroad. The Cold War between the two potential antagonists was thus postponed until both were willing and capable to measure the validity of their ideological credo and the resilience of their respective socio-political systems in the international arena. This moment came when they emerged as the principal victors of the Second World War. It fell on Europe to be the first testing ground for this test of wills and values.

With both Russia and America still in the wings, Europe in the interwar period dominated much, if not most of world politics. It was perhaps a period of last grace. It was certainly badly used when it came to build, or rebuild, a European and international order in the name of collective security, economic recovery and disarmament. The outside world remained either passive or absent or was simply too weak to play any major role in shaping the post-World War I world. In other words: Europe remained more or less sovereign in deciding its own fate and shape. It did not have to defend itself against external pressure. It could pursue its extra-European interests without fear of a major countervailing power except a European rival.

The final reckoning of Europe's place and role in the world was thus kept in abeyance for another twenty-five years. But it came in 1945. The end of the Second World War in fact spelled the definitive end of the kind of Europe that had ruled the waves and the lands for centuries. From its very origins and set-up the United Nations was a different animal than its predecessor, the League. It soon became the locus of an increasingly vituperative debate between the United States and the Soviet Union, both victorious and now confident in the superiority of their ideological mission. There was no hesitation anymore about their global role. They found vigour in their conviction that the other side was evil and doomed. They derived legitimacy for their engagements in the world accusing the other side of aspiring to dominate it. Both derived the principal justification for such accusation from their mutual and growing entanglement in Europe – the continent in whose fratricidal war they had both been drawn by, first, Germany's aggression and, then, her defeat. As allies they occupied, together with Britain and France, Germany and her former allies. As adversaries in the emerging Cold War they faced each other across the Iron Curtain dividing Europe into two opposite camps.

Nothing could have symbolized Europe's demise more than this occupation and partition. For forty years the continent lived in the shadow and with the presence of the two superpowers. For decades it remained under their nuclear umbrella over which it had little or no control. It felt exposed to the whims of Washington and Moscow whose often stormy relationship wavered between mostly collision and occasional collusion. The East European members of the Warsaw Pact had little, if anything to say when it came to formulating military doctrines or foreign policy issues. Moscow's dominance was undisputed. Western Europe on the other hand left if not the decision then the initiative to its American partner. Independent foreign policy making was thus subordinated to either a voluntary or an imposed solidarity that the fight for a common cause demanded. In face of a common adversary this was not felt to be an abdication of national prerogatives. But it prevented the Europeans – both in East and West though in very different ways – to think as Europeans and to act accordingly.

A world divided

Conditions for foreign policy making during the Cold War were therefore very specific, if not unique. Few other regions in the world found themselves in a similar position. This is certainly true for Japan and some of the smaller nations in the Pacific area such as the Koreas, Taiwan as well as Indochina. In other words, the Cold War had its ramifications and prolongation well beyond Europe. At the same time its effect and imprint were far from global. They were certainly not perceived in the same way in most of the countries of the Third World.

The Soviet Union was never a world power in the full meaning of the word – neither economically nor politically, nor even militarily except for its strategic weaponry. It was absent from the main institutions and negotiations in world economy, mostly by its own volition (as in the case of the Marshall Plan) or because its participation was neither desired nor essential. Most of the Soviet Union's client states in the then Third World were economically poor and politically insignificant. The Soviet economic model (if such it was) found few imitators. It failed miserably almost everywhere. The one-party system of Moscovite inspiration owed its durability more to indigenous power than to a desire to install in earnest a proletarian dictatorship. Polycentrism in the communist world found its most glaring expression in the bitter conflict between the two Communist giants, Russia and China. It was proof enough that ideological and political uniformity can at best be enforced on a national and only for some time on the international level.

And yet, the world – and with it the United States and the Soviet Union – came to see the Cold War as a global conflict – and behaved accordingly. From Zhdanov's famous speech in 1947 about the two opposing and irreconcilable camps to President Reagan's rhetoric about the 'evil empire' that should be fought and resisted wherever it raised its head, little doubt was left that mankind was in for a battle of historic proportions. It hardly allowed for neutrality let alone indifference. Nor did it allow for much divergence when it came to taking sides with one or the other camp.

Such vision of unity, solidarity and alignment had the advantage of being convenient and occasionally even profitable. Even the so-called non-aligned countries took advantage of it by playing out one side against the other and often cashing in from whoever was more eager to accommodate. Such vision with its intended simplicity created the illusion of an orderly world, divided into 'good' and 'bad' according to one's perspective. Above all, it had a disciplining effect on allies and alliances, on nearby friends and more distant *protégés*. It conveyed to many countries and regions – which otherwise would have remained at the margins of world politics – the impression of being important and hence entitled to favourable treatment.

Whether or not the Cold War reached all corners of the world seems less important than the way it affected the behaviour of states and the structure of the international order. To the then Soviet Union it gave a sense of importance and respectability which neither its politically repressive system nor its dismal economic performance warranted. Still, in the eyes of the world, it was seen and treated as a world power, on a par with, or certainly a close second to, the United States. Its hegemonic role in Eastern Europe was openly, if grudgingly accepted. Its naval presence on the world's oceans was seen and understood as the natural extension of a power whose strength and influence had traditionally been confined to land.

To the West the confrontation with this expanding and expansionist Soviet Union provided a sense of moral superiority. The values it defended were no doubt the ones that eventually would prevail. At the height of the Cold War this was used, or rather misused, to justify at home a fight against anything that smacked of communism, and abroad to justify the build-up of military alliances and the involvement in distant wars to contain its further expansion. McCarthyism stands for the first, the war in Vietnam for the second. The amount of assistance to a third country was measured less by its invocation of democracy and more by the intensity of its anti-communism. In sum, the Cold War distorted some of the traditional criteria of power and influence. It hastened the process of decolonization in the emerging Third World. It no doubt also propelled the process of integration in Europe. For better or worse, it shaped the world in its own way, according to criteria and perceptions that were either new or had gained a degree of importance that they had never before.

Such development manifested itself in what could be called the social dimension of international politics. The Soviet Union with its leaders from Lenin to Brezhnev introduced the social factor as a determining element in foreign policy. It meant the mobilization of societies as the promoters of socio-political change not just within a state but also beyond its borders. To influence not only the behaviour of states but their societies, to mobilize these societies against their own government, was turned into an integral part of foreign policy. Its spearhead were the omnipresent apparatchiks of the Communist Parties and its supporting cast, the mass movements.

Nowhere was this struggle for the minds and hearts of the people sharper and testier than in Europe. What mattered to the Soviet Union was not merely a gain in the overall balance of power. What mattered was a shift in the 'correlation of forces' that in the Soviet view included, beyond sheer military power and economic resources, the strength and dynamics of the socio-political forces of the given country. Nowhere were such forces claimed to be stronger and superior than in the communist world with its centre, the Soviet Union. Their avantgarde was the working class whom the tide of history would lead to eventual victory. Carried by such certitude the Soviet Union could proclaim that whatever military and financial strength the capitalist world might muster, it was doomed to succumb to these inexorably forward and upward moving forces of communist society. The correlation of forces was therefore proclaimed to change in favour of the East no matter what the West put up for its defence and survival.

Such Soviet sponsored historical determinism was perhaps the strongest force that fuelled the Cold War for decades. Much of it was, to be sure, propaganda. But it held millions under its spell and mobilized mass movements of unheard dimensions. When doubts about the validity of Communist teachings grew more strongly and eventually reached the top echelon of communist leadership under Gorbachev, the end of the Cold War appeared on the horizon: the moment such doubts were allowed to spread, there was little room left to pretending to a socially and morally superior system. The Soviet Union, in other words, lost its ideological claim for a global role and, as a consequence, the legitimacy of playing it.

All this has the ring of a *déjà vu*, a repetition of what we have known already for quite some time. This is correct, of course. But it deserves nevertheless to be repeated because it helps us to understand better the full extent to which the world has changed after the end of the Cold War and the collapse of one of its two principal actors, the Soviet Union.

First, the end of communism spelled also the end of totalitarian ideologies which have so crucially and pervasively characterized the now outgoing twentieth century. In this sense, we can speak of an end of a major chapter of history – a very unfortunate end at that. The disappearance of all-embracing and everything-explaining ideologies, legitimizing every political action – from genocide to totalitarian rule – relieves the world of both a tremendous burden and a constant threat. They no longer serve as justification for and instrument of internal repression and external expansion. Where national interests of states may still clash their pursuit is not vitiated by ideological pretence or political exclusiveness. They are again amenable to accommodation and leave room for compromise. Ideology is no barrier anymore to cooperation with states of different social and political systems; confrontation need not to be permanent because the opposing ideologies are irreconcilable. The superiority of one regime is not judged by the capacity for political mobilization but by the level of economic and social performance.

Back to normal?

In this sense, if in no other, the world is back to normal, to the kind of *Realpolitik* that, as the name implies, is based on constructive cooperation rather than on conditional peaceful coexistence.

In substantive terms, therefore, the parameters of international politics have changed for the better. They were unburdened by the disappearance or death of ideological pretense. Barriers between states and societies were torn down or simply evaporated. Entire libraries of combative pamphlets, solemn declarations and learned works from Marx to Gorbachev, from Mussolini to Hitler, from Mao to Che Guevara became redundant. At best they serve for learned postscripts to a time passed. Some of the ideas may remain or come alive again here or there. But it seems doubtful, so one hopes at least, that they will again serve as the basis and justification of totalitarianism in the murderous and repressive form they took in the twentieth century.

The second major change follows from this first one. It is the logical consequence of the fall of communism and its prime flag-bearer, the

Soviet Union. With the liberation of Central and Eastern Europe and the disintegration of the Soviet Union the bulk of what used to be the Second World disappeared. For almost fifty years it was seen and treated as the socio-political alternative to the first, capitalist world; together they wooed what soon was labelled the Third World – the ideologically and politically not yet committed countries who preferred to stay out of the East-West competition while trying to profit from it.

This numbers' game – and many games with it – was up the moment the Second World had declared its bankruptcy. For all intents and purposes, the communist model as the visiting-card of the Second World disappeared. Of the remaining states which still bear a communist label, none has the power and possibly not even the intention to convert others to their brand of communism. North Korea and Cuba are, if not outcasts, then isolated; China and Vietnam have opened up politically and are undergoing profound economic and social change.

The end of the Second World entailed as its logical consequence also the end of the Third World. As mentioned before, the latter was very much a function of the rivalry between the Capitalist and the Communist ones. Many Third World countries thrived on such rivalry; some, however, also suffered from it. And almost all the newly independent countries derived a good deal of their political identity from it. To all of them, the balance sheet of the Cold War is therefore a mixed one. The legacy of East-West and Soviet-American competition has not just yielded military and economic assistance. It has also brought war and havoc to countries and regions which otherwise would probably have passed an uneventful life on the margins of international politics. Angola, the Horn of Africa and Kampuchea stand as examples.

At the margins is exactly the place where they find themselves today. Whatever strategic or political significance they had in the Cold War, is gone. The fratricidal war in Angola has been going on with all its cruelty and senselessness. Few care about the equally fratricidal civil war in Afghanistan; and Somalia is more or less left again to its own devices, hardly better off after the departure of UN peacekeepers.

Except that – and on many more theatres of East-West rivalry – the only tangible heritage in all these countries is an overabundance of weaponry. Beyond that there is little which could mobilize public attention and great power concern. The continent most affected by this dramatic slip into public oblivion and indifference is Black Africa: a continent in many ways marginalized and in danger of tribalization. The withdrawal of the Soviet Union and the ensuing slackening of interest on part of other extra-regional (mostly industrialized) states has deprived the leaders of many African countries of their external support. It laid open the inefficiency, if not corruption of their respective governments.

Black Africa may be a case of exceptional gravity. But there are other regions which are presently living on the margin. That is true for a number of Central American countries. And it is true for most of the now newly independent republics of the former Soviet Union. In a sense, these two regions live and survive somehow in the shadow of their big neighbours. Each represents in its own way what Moscow calls the 'near abroad': formally independent but in important respects dependent on, and linked to, either Moscow or Washington. The difference to the Cold War period lies in the fact that neither power has any intention – let alone the potential – to intervene effectively in the near abroad of the other. The spectre of Soviet infiltration in Central America and the Caribbean is gone. And so is, except in the minds of the Soviet leadership, if it ever existed, the fear that the United States might penetrate into the Soviet sphere of influence. The long arm of the two world powers, stretching into distant corners of the globe, has been pulled back or, in case of the Soviet Union, simply vanished. The reward for this is a general sense of relief and a feeling of enhanced security: the ever present danger of a nuclear holocaust has, for all intents and purposes, receded into a distant background. The price is benign neglect, if not total indifference, *vis-à-vis* now derelict regions that only a few years ago seemed to be precisely the focus or detonator of such conflagration.

This leads us directly to the third consequence of the Cold War's end. With it the world has lost – for better or worse – some organizing principles, some rules of the game that helped us to move from dangerous confrontation to acceptable coexistence, to avoid major and catastrophic wars and to develop some procedures for controlling an ever escalating arms race. Nobody will glorify such achievements which owe their existence more to mutual fear than to shared wisdom. But they did attenuate some excesses. They kept a lid on some risks and limited the extent of several crises.

For all intents and purposes, such a 'disciplining' effect has disappeared. The rivalry of the erstwhile superpowers does no longer shape international politics or distort national interests. Ideological loyalty is no longer a yardstick for the extent of military protection and economic assistance. Nor is it anymore a barrier to dialogue and cooperation between countries with different political outlooks and different internal regimes.

But somewhat facetiously: with all the manifold ideological barriers, political considerations and strategic engagements either gone or now redundant, the world finds itself in a different ball game of a 'free for all'. Germany can deal with Russia without being immediately suspected of reviving the spirit of Rapallo; Washington can talk to formerly black-listed Syria not about terrorism but making peace with Israel. South Africa has moved out of its isolation and become an important partner of Black Africa; and the PLO has concluded a first important peace agreement with Israel.

All this is undoubtedly good and welcome. But such 'free for all' and 'everybody with everybody' can have its price. The price would seem to be the rapid disappearance of all or most rules of the game. Sanctions for those who violate them, hardly exist anymore or, if applied, have little effect. The great powers have relinquished all or most of global responsibility or engagement that they thought was necessary during the Cold War. Now they conduct foreign affairs like anybody else geared by national, i.e. purely domestic interests. Arms control agreements are no longer a priority. Little pressure is left actually to implement or complement them. The concern for what used to be called 'international security' has noticeably declined, first, because the danger of an international war has receded, second, because it has become difficult to agree on what security in an interdependent world means and by what or by whom it is threatened. As a consequence, the belief in an all-redeeming system of collective security has rapidly faded, the Gulf war probably remaining a unique experience. The instruments or institutions for regional security are either still in their infancy or, as in Europe, turned out to be of little use when it comes to dealing with internal conflicts and parties – be they drug cartels, irregular rebel forces or frustrated minorities. They rather than external foes would seem to pose a security threat both to states and societies. To deal with them will mean transferring the battle for order from the international to the national or even local arena; it will mean adjusting the peace-keeping missions of international organizations to the new requirements of a rapidly changing environment.

Admittedly, most universal organizations were either fully or partly paralyzed by the freezing atmosphere of the Cold War. They still fulfilled the mission of maintaining a dialogue between the antagonists and of providing a framework within which compromises could be worked out. Perhaps this and other mediating functions of international organizations during the Cold War and their influence on the behaviour of the national actors are underestimated. On the other hand, their present potential for fostering consensus and strengthening collective action is probably overestimated. They are victims of a resurgence of national interests that every country – be it big or small, central or peripheral – can now pursue more freely and more recklessly than under the more demanding and harsher conditions of the postwar years.

All this needs not be a cause for nostalgia for a now bygone era. For all practical purposes it was an era of a senseless, costly and dangerous arms race, of futile clashes of faith and vanity, of vastly wasteful engagements in distant regions and of hegemonic aspirations. When all this came to an end, the world did not simply return to normal. Too many things had changed. Technology, communications and mobility, the flow of capital and the reach of weaponry, the uneasy coexistence of abundant wealth with abject poverty and last but not least, the growth of population and the decline of the environment. All this and much more is constantly modifying the nature, intensity and direction of world politics. The Cold War was an episode and a very crucial one at that. But its end still leaves us with these many new factors and actors. They, much more than some of the failures and errors of the Cold War itself, will shape the course of the world of tomorrow. Europe as the main theatre of East-West confrontation is experiencing this more than any other continent.

II. The Changing Landscape in Europe

It is not just the outside world which has profoundly changed. It is also Europe. Nowhere was – and still is – the Cold War's imprint deeper and more lasting than on the European continent. It has undergone transformation of historic dimensions. Inevitably some of this transformation is due to the Cold War and its legacy. But not all. There is also a return to, or of history, frozen under the blanket of Soviet domination, cut off at its roots by the continent's political and military division, or hidden by a seemingly unending economic growth that almost all of a sudden came to a halt and thus re-awakened time-honoured anxieties about social security and personal protection.

The continent is no longer divided. The fall of the Berlin wall is more than a symbolic testimony to this. Europe's geography changed. Above all, it expanded. An important part of what in the Cold War jargon was labelled 'Eastern Europe' moved back to its former central place. It is Central Europe again with the united Germany as its major and most important part. As a consequence, France, for forty years the prime centre and mover of (West)European integration, found herself suddenly on the continent's Western periphery. And so did, in a similar but even more pronounced way, the countries of Southern Europe, Spain and Portugal in particular. Great Britain had, wisely but perhaps not always helpfully, stayed somewhat aloof by keeping one foot in the Commonwealth and one arm across the Atlantic.

On the other side of the continent developments were and are more dramatic and complex. The overdue break-down of forty years of communist rule in Central and Eastern Europe and the totally unexpected break-up of its long-time master, the Soviet Union, brought these regions back into the 'normal' circuit of European politics. At the same time it opened up the vast spaces of Russia reaching well into Central Asia and the Far East. This seemingly unending land is, however, littered with the spoils and failures of a system that treated man and nature recklessly. It caused mental and environmental damage of unheard proportions. The fifteen republics of the former Soviet Union became almost overnight independent states.

The three Baltic republics regained what had been a shortlived independence in the interwar period. All the others now form a periphery around the Russian centre. None of them is economically really viable because their economy was conceived and constructed as part of the highly centralized Soviet state. Nor have they carried out the kind of political reform that would open the way to a somewhat stable democratic system. They stopped halfway, torn between relying on old and experienced communist guards and the necessity of reform, between a natural desire for political independence of, and a historical return to, Moscow.

Russia and Europe

The future of this new East is and will remain for many years uncertain. It is fragmented and unstable.[11] The place and role of Russia are far from being defined. Russia has undergone a process of both geographical and strategic retrenchment. It leaves many, if not most Russians in doubt about their 'Europeaness'. Today's Russia has no borders anymore with Central and Southern Europe. It is still a neighbour of Finland in the West and Turkey in the South. In other words: it has moved to the periphery of the continent, half part of it but hardly belonging to it. Russians have lost what, after the Second World War, they had seen as their main mission, namely being at the same time the principal guarantor of European order and the future alternative to its doomed

11 Cf. Table I in the annex.

Western part. This double mission, however threatening to foes and unyielding for allies never came to pass. Its disappearance leaves a void that the country and its people will sooner or later want to fill again. The great question is how and with what content the void is going to be filled and what this will mean for Russia herself and for Europe as a whole.

For the time being the situation is in full flux. This is particularly true for the new and hastily created CIS. It is artificial in substance and most likely short-lived in time – at least in its present shape. Most of the now independent former Soviet republics remain oriented to, if not dependent on, Russia. That applies even to the Ukraine and certainly to Central Asia and the Caucasus. All these new states carry the burden and responsibility of a communist past with its established rules and rulers. Some have gone further in their – mostly limited – political and economic reforms than others. Some resuscitate local traditions and pride themselves of a history of their own. Others are artificial creations of Stalinist making. While being formal members of the OSCE many stay aloof from its political credo and its daily activities.

Still, the fact remains that, officially or institutionally, these distant countries with their uncertain future are considered to be part of the enlarged Europe. By and through their membership with the OSCE on the one hand, the North Atlantic Cooperation Council (NAAC) and, for some, the Partnership for Peace on the other, they are linked to institutions whose central objective is to make the 'new' countries respect the guidelines and principles laid down in the Helsinki Act of 1975 and the Paris Charter of 1990. One can have doubts whether and how far the countries are able and willing to do so. There are several conflicts if not outright wars going on in some CIS states. Armenia is embroiled in a conflict with Azerbaijan about Nagorno Karabakh. Tajikistan is suffering from a disruptive and often bloody civil war. And so is Georgia where internal strife for power is mixed with secessionist fights in Abkazia and Ossetia. The Republic of Chechnya, after having declared its independence from the Russian Federation, is being brought to heel by Moscow's brutal onslaught and occupation.

In all this, and in much more, Russia is playing the role of either arbiter or policeman, or both at the same time. The Russian army behaves as a self-appointed peace-keeper – a role it has assumed also in Transdnjestria claimed by Moldova as part of its territory. The Crimea, handed over to Ukraine by Krushchev in 1954, is torn by opposite loyalties – Tartars returning from exile being anti-Russian, the local Russian population opting for Moscow, and Ukraine claiming its legal rights for the unfortunate peninsula. In the North East, the three Baltic states have regained full independence after the last Russian soldier departed from their territory in 1994.

Such a brief *tour d'horizon* is nothing more than a double reminder: first, that the apparently 'monolithic' and highly centralized Soviet Union was in fact an empire, and a colonial one at that. More than any other empire it has dominated, if not standardized and certainly centralized its colonies or dominions. It could do so not only because of its own totalitarian system but also because of the geographic proximity of these colonialized territories. In other words, Russian imperialism was directed at the 'near' and not at a 'far' abroad. It was – and still is – more geographic than ethnic or religious, more of a territorial conquest than economics or trade which determined the direction and fuelled the drive of Russian expansionism. Unlike the European colonial powers, Russia and its successor, the Soviet Union, did not have to go overseas to acquire influence and wealth: it found them at its doorstep. Here as much as in the oppressive nature of the political regime lies the main reason why the Soviet Union was able to keep control over these territories, much longer than the other colonial powers of Europe.

Perhaps this helps to explain why the Soviet Union came to an abrupt end not by a war but almost peacefully. The world stood by. It watched with awe this unexpected historic event but did not try to exploit it let alone grab the spoils of the sunken ship. What came in its wake was, and still is, less peaceful. As pointed out before, there are conflicts and tensions in the former Soviet Union. Above all there is no assurance whatsoever that such tranquillity will last and that Europe, for the remains of the day, can count with a fairly stable and self-contained East, be it Russia or, further afield, the Transcaucasus and Central Asia.

46

The Eastern arc of hopes and crises

The West of this East, i.e. Central and Eastern European countries, has different perspectives and different problems. These countries find themselves once more in search of identity – national, cultural and other. Their overall orientation is westwards. It points towards, first, the European Union and, second, the North Atlantic with its established defence and security structure, i.e. NATO. Economic viability, political stability and military security are those countries' obvious and natural objectives. Each of them is difficult to attain. But all of them converge in the desire of assistance from, and attachment to what used to be called, in Cold War times, the West. Poland, the Czech Republic, Slovakia, Hungary, and Romania have new-old neighbours. It is no longer the overpowering Soviet Union. It is Lithuania, Belarus, Ukraine and Moldova, newly independent states whose future status does not seem fully assured. They cannot offer either economic assistance or military security or political stability. But they are important both as trade partners and as buffers between these countries and Russia.

The linchpin or bedrock in this now again Eastern-oriented *cordon sanitaire* is Ukraine. With its 52 million inhabitants and a surface of over 600,000 km² it is the first new middle power to appear on the continent since the reunification of Germany and Italy in the 19th century. Given a healthy economy and a minimum of political stability, Ukraine could become an important player in the new Europe. In the positive sense it could serve as a stabilizer in a strategically sensitive area, as a transit route for Russian oil and gas, and as a supplier of both agricultural and industrial products. In a negative sense Ukraine's re-integration into a reconstituted and enlarged Russia might set Europe's strategic clock back to either 1914 or 1939 – making Russia again the immediate neighbour of Central and Eastern Europe. Politically and economically this might just be acceptable if such a Russian neighbour had a democratic regime and an open economy. But even then, Europe would have to reconsider the ways and means by which such a reconstitution or control of a central part of Eastern Europe's strategic landscape could be kept secure and stable.

Europe's second problem area is the South East or the Balkans. Its focus is, or was, Yugoslavia. But it neither begins nor ends there. In historical, cultural and ethnic terms it stretches from Croatia to Turkey, from the Adriatic to the Black Sea. A highly heterogeneous area therefore, if ever there was one. An area with a long historical memory and a long and painful record of conflict and wars, occupation and oppression. The Yugoslav tragedy has opened many of the barely healed wounds of previous times. It laid open the vulnerability of the region to mutual recrimination, religious mistrust and ethnic clivages.

It may be that the ongoing civil war can be contained and eventually ended. Even then we cannot be sure that its underlying causes will really be eliminated. And nobody can, or should, exclude a spillover of the conflict into neighbouring areas nor indeed the possibility of new conflicts. Precisely because the Balkans were viewed, and treated, by the main European powers as a – mostly unpleasant – sideshow of 'grand European politics' they were not included into major peacemaking efforts, let alone attempts at integration.

The Yugoslav conflict was thus allowed to escalate into a drama probably nobody would have thought possible after the end of the Cold War. But Europe's incapacity to understand and anticipate this drama and its impotence to deal with it, clearly proves that the Balkans are still considered as peripheral. To many they still appear as a side-show. They may move us morally, but they are not considered as an area for which major powers feel obliged to risk a major confrontation. The question therefore remains valid whether the Balkan countries should and can be made a full part of European concerns, whether they ought to be included institutionally and integrated politically and economically as equal and equally valuable partners. Obviously they should. But the obstacles are enormous. And so is the risk that once parts or all of the Balkans have found their place within the European Union, they may still remain a source of constant friction.

A turbulent South

The third area of concern is Europe's South. By this we mean the Mediterranean in general, and North Africa in particular. It is in many ways and in spite of a long era of European colonial rule, a different world: Arabic and Muslim, both having different traditions, outlooks and expectations. In spite of many similarities, each country from western-most Morocco to Syria in the Middle East, is different in size, political constitution and foreign policy interests. They have however a few features in common that must interest if not worry Europe.[12]

The following comparison between the population of the EU Mediterranean members and the non-EU states in the Mediterranean shows the shifting balance.

	Inhabitants in millions	
	1995	2010
European Union (15 member states)	368 m	399 m
Mediterranean members of European Union*	165 m	178 m
Non-EU Mediterranean countries**	213 m	304 m

* France, Greece, Italy, Spain
** Morocco, Algeria, Libya, Tunisia, Egypt, Israel, Lebanon, Syria, Turkey

The first feature has to do with demographic growth. As the above table shows the population of all countries has dramatically increased over the last thirty years. Between 55 and 65 percent of the people in the Arab countries are under 24 years old. This contrasts sharply with Europe's ageing population. Here, those under twenty years old make up hardly more than one quarter, at best thirty percent. One may rejoice in the continuing rejuvenation of the Southern rim of the Mediterranean and deplore the ageing of the Europeans. But the possible consequences of such a tectonic shift in the population structure will have

12 Cf. Research Group on European Affairs, Challenges in the Mediterranean – The European Response, Gütersloh 1991; and Table II in the annex.

far-reaching consequences for both the political stability and the economic development of its Southern littoral.

This leads to the second consideration, i.e. the serious economic situation of many, if not most of the North African countries. They share the problems associated with demographic growth and high unemployment on the one hand, and low or slow economic growth on the other. Together these factors make either for social tension at home or encourage emigration, or both at the same time. Algeria's current social and political unrest is spurred by fundamentalist forces. Perhaps it is an extreme case. Whether Islamic religious fanaticism in its various forms and manifestations will spread is difficult to say. Where its message is that of greater care for the poor, and a revival of religious belief, it may find fertile and receptive ground in some of the Arab-Muslim countries. Almost fatally, such awakening and strengthening of Islamic forces contains a more or less combative streak of anti-Westernism, a condemnation of Western materialism and values. Such 'fundamentalist' critique of the existing socio-political regimes at home and of an often overbearing Western influence from abroad is not without justification. The tragedy, however, is that many of its protagonists have come to the conclusion that such critique will only be heard and heeded if accompanied by the threat or actual use of force. Almost fatally this will turn them into revolutionary movements, i.e. movements willing or driven to resort to force where they come to the conclusion that peaceful change is impossible under present circumstances. Few, if any of the Arab countries can boast regimes that allow for more than cosmetic change by peaceful and democratic means. They are politically conservative and institutionally authoritarian. Mindful of what radical fundamentalism has done to countries like Iran and Sudan they resist Islamic movements, even if moderate. These are perceived as a threat to the existing order. A clash, actual or potential, between the forces in being and those in the making, the official defenders of the status quo and opposition groups who want to change it, thus seems to be foreordained. Algeria is the first in Northern Africa to experience it in the most brutal way. Few would dare to predict that it will remain the only one.

Paradoxically, the cultural and religious divide between the Northern and the Southern Mediterranean may therefore become sharper at the same time as the need for a more concerted economic and social cooperation becomes greater. Neither side can ignore the other. But so far they seem to have found little common ground for a sustained and mutually helpful dialogue. There were, of course, various sorts of agreements, bilateral and multilateral. The European Community has repeatedly initiated a dialogue and formulated what can be called a Mediterranean policy. To inject into such a heterogenous region anything like a coherent and sustainable policy over a prolonged period of time, is difficult indeed. And yet, it would seem that such a policy becomes unavoidable if this third 'peripheral region' is not to become one more and serious concern to Europe's own security and stability. To this we will have to return below.

Europe's uncertainties

At the end of this more than perfunctory overview of Europe's immediate geographic, political and economic neighbourhood, some brief conclusions are in place. They will take us to the question about the instruments and methods the European Union has at its disposal – or in fact may have not – to face up to this changing geopolitical landscape.

The first conclusion would seem obvious: Europe in its various political and geographic configurations has become – again – a multifacetted, if not volatile continent. This means that its future is less predictable than it has been during the seemingly endless confrontation and division during the Cold War. There are few principles that the 54 member countries of the OSCE will adhere to loyally and equally. Still, the OSCE has its rules and stipulations. The problem with them is that they convey the impression of an orderly and well organized continent, with more, and more durable, institutions.[13] This is more than any other continent (North America with three states only is a special case) can boast of. But nobody can be sure whether, in time of need, they

13 Cf. Table III in the annex.

will actually be observed. Figuratively speaking, this enlarged and over-institutionalized Europe is a *trompe l'oeil* – a splendid and colourful hall with beautiful sculptures which, at closer scrutiny, reveal themselves as having no depth and little substance.

The second conclusion relates to Europe's present fragmentation on the one hand, and the slackening movement towards integration on the other. The often heard juxtaposition of 'fragmentation in the East' and 'integration in the West' may become misleading. Misleading in a double sense: first, because the process of fragmentation seems to have come to a halt, the possible exception being a further disintegration or fractionalization of former Yugoslavia. On the other hand, we observe various signs of a rapprochement between several members of the Commonwealth of Independent States and its centre, Russia. It may be premature to call it anything like a reconstitution of the Czarist or Soviet empire. But it would seem that the move 'away from Moscow' has not only slowed down but, for political and economic reasons, may be reversing. Europe may still be fragmented, both in an institutional and political sense. But nobody can tell how deep and permanent this fragmentation is, nor do we know whether it will turn into a serious obstacle to further integration or simply reflect more adequately the immense diversity of a continent that has never experienced true unity.

The third conclusion is that Europe is again a very heterogeneous and disorderly continent. Different levels of economic development and social security exist side by side. There is still a deep institutional imbalance between the 'Eastern' and the 'Western' part of Europe. The former has abolished its Soviet-sponsored institutions, the latter has retained and further expanded its own. The OSCE is so far the only all-embracing but still very fragile European institution. To be sure, there is the North Atlantic Cooperation Council and the Partnership for Peace. They both are NATO-sponsored and thus of Western origin. And so will be, of course, any enlargement of the European Union and NATO eastwards. There are already various treaties of association between the European Union and several Central and Eastern European countries. Together, they are no doubt welcome initiatives, appreciated by those who have accepted them. But they have neither an equivalent in the East nor are they considered by these countries to be adequate. They therefore do not satisfy their expectations because they do not cater to their security concerns in a strategically fluid environment.

Such a Europe with its resurfaced diversity defies any clear geographic definition or delimitation. It has no moral centre of gravity and few points of political reference that would provide the basis for its future organization. That need not be bad in itself. One of Europe's characteristics has always been its diversity. Unfortunately this has also been the reason for its weakness. Diversity was the midwife of wars but is hardly that of integration. Hence the concepts of federalism and, more recently, of subsidiarity. But both require longstanding experience and innumerable compromises. Both again can be an element of weakness as much as of one of strength.

The fourth conclusion follows from the previous one. With Europe's organization in flux, new constellations of power and influence may, and probably will, emerge. As territorial conquest is, barring minor exceptions, no longer a source of conflict, we can assume that a major international war on the continent is highly unlikely. But economic power, financial desequilibria, internal unrest and political clout remain moving forces in intra-European relations. They can lead to the formation of new or the dissolution of existing units. They can lead to shifts in the distribution of power. They can cause new antagonisms or revive old ones. Nobody would wish to exclude the re-emergence of Russia or a reconstituted Russian empire of sorts. It would be too big for inclusion into the expanding European Union but also too big to be left outside. It may become a power centre in its own right. As such it may be instrumental in recreating a new and hopefully peaceful and stable balance of power with those states that constitute the European Union of whatever composition and cohesion. In sum then, the political structure and stability of Europe will remain subject to change and shifts. Their effects we do not know yet. But they will have to be taken into account in any forecast of Europe's future.

The fifth and final conclusion has to do with what we called Europe's peripheries. They encompass the regions which lie outside the European Union, the latter being understood here as the nucleus from which major impulses for Europe's future order will hopefully come. Irrespective of whether or not the Union will eventually include all or most European states, its responsibility for, or interest in, these regions will remain central for its own existence. Hence a continuing, nay growing need to pay attention to these regions. Each requires a different and differentiated policy – ranging from the strengthening of bilateral relations to a treaty of association or partnership, from aid to political cooperation and dialogue. It is no doubt a daunting task: to face up to an East where Russia expects us to live with her ambivalent policy, towards what she still calls her 'near abroad' and hence constantly shifting power relations within the Commonwealth of Independent States; to a South-East where we anxiously observe the resurgence of the treaty of Westphalia's principle *cuius regio eius religio;* and to a South, torn between political authoritarianism and social-religious radicalism.

Europe is thus left with what we may call 'the eight uncertainties':

- the uncertainty about the future of the Russian Federation both with regard to the direction and fate of its economic reforms and to the nature of its political regime and overall cohesion as a federation;
- the uncertainty about the structure of the Commonwealth of Independent States, torn between the necessity of a closer cooperation of its members with the dominating power of Russia and their desire to maintain national independence;
- the uncertainty about Russia's position in and relationship with the rest of Europe (and the United States), particularly if an eastwards enlargement of NATO is not compensated by a corresponding agreement with Russia. In such a case Europe may be heading again for another kind of division with an expanded Alliance on one side, and a marginalized Russia as the centre of a reconstituted Commonwealth of States on the other;
- the uncertainty about the future status of the Central and East European states and their capacity to develop an efficient and stable administration;
- the uncertainty about the outcome of the war in former Yugoslavia and the fate and future of countries like Serbia and Turkey;
- the uncertainty about the future socio-political development of the Southern Mediterranean littoral and the Middle East peace process;

- the uncertainty about the consequences of a further enlargement of the European Union and the likelihood of its internal reform; and finally,
- the uncertainty about the future role, size and interaction of the existing organizations in Europe in charge of defence and/or security (NATO, WEU, OSCE and CIS) and the nature of conflict they may have to deal with in the future.

It is a landscape that outsiders look at with bewilderment. Europe is suddenly seen no longer as a continent of stability, security and expanding integration. Rather it appears as a region where armed conflict seems possible again, where borders can be once more put into question, and where the old spectre of nationalism re-emerges as a challenge, if not as an obstacle to more integration. How then can the European Union assemble enough strength and cohesion to make use of its tremendous potential both for its own good and that of the international community?

III. The Instruments of Power

Looked at from the outside, the European Union appears as an important player on the international arena. Of course, it is but in its own way, for at least three mutually reinforcing reasons. First, the Community turned Union represents probably the most innovative and successful concept of intra-state cooperation, reconciliation and eventually integration in the postwar era. Second, and as a consequence of this, the Union has over the years become the world's most important trade power. And third and most recently, the Union, as a political entity with its own bureaucratic apparatus and diplomatic machinery has become, after the end of Europe's division, the central pillar and point of orientation on a continent of some fifty states.

The question, then, is whether the European Union will be able to live up to the manifold expectations addressed to it. To be a power and act as one requires more than a continuing growth in wealth and membership. Power in the traditional sense presupposes more. To be credible in purpose and enduring in effect it needs a centre of political decision-making, a common political will and the appropriate instruments that make the latter come to pass.

Economic power at large

None of these three factors is present at the moment. The Union derives its 'power' – if such it is – and influence from other sources. First and foremost from its very existence as an institution that has stood the test of time and trial. Second, as a multilayered institution supported by a huge bureaucracy, the Commission, and an ever spreading network of diplomatic missions of which many states may well be envious. Third, there is the Union's economic potential allowing for innumerable programmes and agreements of assistance and advice.

All this is unique. It is therefore important in its own right. It may not be measurable in terms of political clout or military hardware. But it has, above and beyond its economic and financial dimension, a very special psychological impact on people and states. Because it conveys the perception that the Union, its manifold weaknesses and shortcomings notwithstanding, is an institution with a future. In contrast to many, if not most of the institutions born out of the Cold War, the European Union has not outlived itself and its usefulness. If there was disappointment about its performance – or rather non-performance – in the Yugoslav drama, it was due largely, though surely not only, to exaggerated expectations about its political if not military capacity. By its very constitution, it simply was unable to meet these expectations. This is not an exculpation for past mistakes. It is an explanation for still glaring insufficiencies.

Why, then, still this enduring image of a union that, far from having lost its mission, is expected to fulfill an ever greater one in the years to come? Perhaps the most important reason – surely not the only one – has to do with the profound changes in the international environment in which the Union finds itself. In other words: if it has an important future it is not simply attributable to its own merits and performance. It is due to the fact that the Union's very domain – economics – has moved up to the top place of the international agenda. This may or may not be healthy for the international political order, for the prevention of armed conflicts and the protection of the environment. It is still a fact. The globalization of the economy and the emergence of regional economic blocs overshadow almost everywhere the need for political cooperation and for the promotion of security and defence institutions.

Such a secular trend, already detectable in the last stages of the Cold War, became openly visible after the senseless and fruitless East-West confrontation had ended. With it ended, at least on the intra-state level, much of a no less senseless arms race, both nuclear and conventional. Military strength as the determining factor in the international power equation lost some of its relevance. And so did ideological competition and the political wooing of friends or clients. It simply fuelled the militarization of many parts of the world dividing it in spheres of influence and affluence. Much, surely not all of this came to an end when the Soviet bloc recognized that its strategic overstretch had undermined its economic base, and when the Soviet Union itself ended its seventy years' existence with a break-down as a viable political system and with a break-up as an artificial federation. Together, this double *finale* relegated the importance of the military to a second or third rank position. With it went the concern about defence and security. Its place was taken by a no less vivid concern for economic performance and social well-being. The former was spurred by growing economic global competition, the latter by the spectre of international migration and national unemployment. The victims of this shift were the various international institutions which had catered to the political stability and military defence. They are now searching for a new mission or have to declare themselves redundant.

The European Union finds itself in the mainstream of this change. It is perceived as an institution that, from its very beginning, had put economic reconstruction and integration as its first and foremost objectives. It achieved unexpected results by creating, for the first time, a single common market and ending up so far with a treaty for an economic and political union. As such it should be well-equipped to face up to the numerous challenges, both internal and external, of a new and more demanding environment. No wonder, then, that it soon found itself bombarded with requests for aid and assistance and a lengthening queue of states applying or at least hoping for membership.

Such new interest and all too flattering admiration are no doubt a boost to the occasionally sagging morale of the Union and its often criticized officials. The question remains whether all these hopes and expectations are not a Danean gift: the Union is expected to do more than, in its present constitution, it will be able to deliver. Our analysis of the changing international environment shows that it finds itself in a world in which more than economic power and financial assistance – even if both are crucial – is expected from it.

From this follow crucial and possibly embarrassing questions: will the European Union be able to meet these new and wider expectations? Will it be given the means to become the kind of actor that the reconstruction and consolidation of Europe actually need? And: will it be able to act politically in a way that corresponds to its economic power? The last question may in fact reveal that the dividing line between power and impotence is perilously thin. It is here where the litmus test will have to be passed to see whether impressive economic power will generate a modicum of political responsibility in these final years of a turbulent century. The world at large and Europe in particular may need both.

A panoply of agreements

For the moment a brief overview of some of the main instruments may give an idea of the power, or power potential, of the European Union. Nobody would deny that they are not impressive. We have here to do with an association or club of states which, in an historically novel way, have achieved very much. It is surely much more than even the greatest optimist would have thought possible when the Treaty of Rome was solemnly signed almost forty years ago.

Since then, the Union has developed a full panoply of instruments and mechanisms to promote the economies of its members. As a result, trade grew both among them and with an ever widening number of third countries. Today, the Union can bring into play, on various levels and in various directions, the assets that its *acquis communautaire*, i.e. the accumulated set of agreements, institutions and integrated areas, has assembled and brought to fruit. And it can offer a wide range of financial assistance to countries in need.[14]

Whatever the value of statistics may be, there is no denying that the European Union is now the world's most important trading power. In

14 Cf. Table IV in the annex.

1993 its share of world trade was 20 percent. Its external exports (excluding the intercommunity trade) amounted to more than ECU 430 billion in 1992. The members accounted for 15 percent of world exports compared with 12 percent for the United States, 9 percent for Japan and some 12 percent for the rest of Asia.[15]

The Union's trade pattern is still rather one-sided. Over half of its exports (intra-Union trade again excluded) went to other highly industrialized countries (at that time the still functioning EFTA, United States and Canada as well as Japan). Only little trade was done with Latin America and even less with Africa. In the last few years, the emerging markets in Asia moved up on the list of trading partners, China being the most important and, to many, also the most promising partner. Many barriers to a free flow of goods still exist on both sides. The entering into force of the new global trade agreements – under the auspices of the equally new World Trade Organization (WTO) – will remove many of these barriers. An expansion of trade will follow, and, according to present calculations, the Union will be amongst its greatest beneficiaries.[16]

The Union is the biggest market in the industrialized world with a population, after its fourth enlargement, of some 368 million. It would be daring indeed to underestimate, let alone ignore its tremendous purchasing power. To be sure, in sheer numbers, it represents only one third or soon only one quarter of China's population (1.2 bn). But its per capita income is about ten times higher. This gap may gradually become smaller. But it will remain both an economic and a political fact of life for years to come.

It was both its colonial heritage and its fierce rivalry with the Communist world that directed the Community's economic policy first and foremost south- and westwards, i.e. to the newly independent and other developing countries on the one hand, and to the partners and allies in North America on the other. As regards the developing countries, the Community made a conscious effort to devise ways and means for supporting their political stabilization and economic devel-

---

15 Cf. European Commission, The European Union and World Trade, Brussels, June 1995.
16 Cf. Table V in the annex.

opment. It steadily increased the proportion of its budget devoted to aid and international support. The Union today is the principal provider of foreign direct investment and provides 53 percent of all official development assistance. The main instrument for the latter are the Lomé Agreements with their by now four up-dated versions. With 69 developing countries as signatories they present the largest single aid programme in the world. The most recent (fourth) Convention (1990–2000) provides for 12 bn ECU in the form of grants, soft loans and interest rate rebates.[17]

Besides these substantial commitments – hardly enough in the eyes of many, particularly poor countries – the most interesting feature of the latest Lomé Agreement is its political dimension. For the first time the Community/Union could raise, so to speak, the political stakes in exchange for its economic aid. Recipient countries are now being asked (as it is clearly stated in the Preamble of the Single Act of 1987) "to display the principles of democracy and compliance with the law and with human rights to which they are attached, so that together they may make their own contribution to the preservation of international peace and security".

These objectives clearly go beyond a simple expansion of trade or offer of aid. They imply that by concluding agreements to this purpose the Union and its members also have a *political* purpose in mind. In this sense, the agreements are aimed at the promotion of democracy and at the better protection of human rights in the partner country. Such linkage between economic aid and political performance comes close to what the United States as a superpower practised since the Carter presidency – if not before. The message is clear: the economically stronger can impose on the economically more needy and the politically 'less correct' some of its own standards. It is, what today is openly and correctly called, a 'policy of conditionality': the stronger and wealthier attach specific conditions to its aid. Today, such policy can be applied more freely as the principal rival, the Soviet Union, has disappeared as the only powerful though economically hardly persua-

17 Günter Burghardt, The European Union's Role in Tomorrow's World, unpublished text of a lecture prepared for the 1995 'Seminar on International Security' in Geneva.

sive alternative. Receiving countries can therefore no longer threaten to turn to Moscow if they feel that Western countries (or indeed the Community) press them too harshly. What is left to them is no longer a choice between opposing political systems, but between different versions of market economy, each of them insisting on the respect of similar if not identical political values.

No doubt: the absence of a political opponent makes it easier for the Community to get across not just its economic aid and advice but also its political message. As mentioned before, this finds already its reflection in the fourth Lomé Agreement of December 1989. At the same time it enhances the Community's responsibility both as regards the formulation of its own political philosophy and vis-à-vis its current and future partners. Nowhere did this double responsibility become more evident than when Brussels had to define its policy vis-à-vis Central and Eastern Europe, emerging from forty years of Soviet domination and expecting support from, and rapid association with, Western Europe.

Here now was a challenge of a totally new order. It was as unexpected as it was delicate. The Union had to try, and is still trying, to come to grips with it on four levels. They correspond more or less to the internal situation of the Central and East European countries and countries of the former Soviet Union, their geographical location and, linked to this, their historical and cultural affinities with Western Europe. The Union tackled this new task with the appropriate nuances. First, it concluded 'Europe agreements'.[18] Presently (1995) such agreements were concluded with ten countries: Poland, Czech Republic, Slovakia, Hungary, Romania, Bulgaria, Estonia, Latvia, Lithuania and Slovenia.

The agreements provide for free trade (though with notable exceptions in sectors like agriculture, textiles and steel). They also include economic and technical cooperation as well as financial assistance. It is understood that these ten countries adopt the central principles of market economy and guarantee their citizens those democratic and human rights to which not only the Union members adhere but which

18   Cf. Table VI in the annex.

were solemnly consecrated by the Paris Charter of the CSCE in 1990. Here again we find the linkage between economics and politics. The Union, more than any other Western or European institution, sees itself entitled to insist on this link as it possesses what none of these other institutions do, namely economic and financial leverage for the attainment of political objectives.

The European Council, at its meeting in June 1993, decided that countries tied to the Union with a Europe agreement could expect to become full members if they met a series of conditions. First, they must have established stable institutions guaranteeing democracy, the rule of law, human rights and respect for, and protection of, minorities. Second, they must prove the existence of a functioning market economy. Third, they must have the capacity to cope with competitive pressure and market forces within the Union. And finally, they must be prepared to take on the obligations of membership (the *acquis communautaire*), including adherence to the Union's objectives of political, economic and monetary union.

These are stiff conditions indeed. They were spelled out in more detail in a 'White Paper' which the European Commission published in May 1995.[19] The White Paper forms, in its own words, "part of the pre-accession strategy for the associated countries of Central and Eastern Europe . . . Its purpose is to provide a guide to assist (these countries) in preparing themselves for operating under the requirements of the European Union's internal market". It identifies a long list of key measures in each sector of that market. But according to the White Paper, taking these measures will not be enough. There must also be adequate structures capable of implementing and, if need be, enforcing these measures.

Several conclusions can be drawn from these stipulations. First, they clearly show that the Union is not the demandeur in its relationship with Central and Eastern Europe. While obviously offering the associated countries its assistance and guidance, it is the Union which calls the tune and sets the conditions. A second conclusion could be that the

19 White Paper on Preparation of the Associated Countries of Central and Eastern Europe for Integration into the Internal Market of the Union. Commission of the European Union, Brussels, 3 May 1995.

Union is in no particular hurry to receive new and potentially unstable countries, the support of which will constitute an additional and serious drain on the Union's budget. One might go even so far as to see in the White Paper more of a barrier to than an invitation for entry. All this shows, third, that the Union is determined to preserve its *acquis communautaire* even if in a few years it will count some 20 or 25 members. This means that the Union sees itself as the overarching roof under which the majority of the European countries, from Portugal to Poland, can assemble and coalesce.

A second major category of agreements is of a different, more strategic nature: the Union's relationship with the states of the former Soviet Union in general and Russia in particular. Even before the former's breakdown, in 1990, the Union explored possibilities of elaborating a broadly based agreement with Moscow, going beyond the Trade and Cooperation Agreement concluded the year before (December 1989).

Behind this intention was the clear recognition that the Soviet Union or its main successor, the Russian Federation, would remain an important player on the European scene.[20] Hence, Europe as a whole, and the Union in particular, had and still has every interest in assisting Russia and the CIS in their ambitious economic reforms seen as a precondition for political stability.

The result of these considerations were negotiations on Partnership and Cooperations Agreements (PCA) with the aim of providing cooperation in political economic and technical issues. Corresponding agreements with Russia and the Ukraine were signed in June 1994. Here again, advice and assistance does not come free even if the trade between the Union and the CIS is flourishing. But the Union has made it quite clear that it hopes that Russia, Ukraine and the other CIS members will move towards market economy and democracy, and vouch for the observance of human rights. It is because of doubts about the latter – as a consequence of Russia's military intervention in Chechnya – that the PCA with Russia has not yet entered into force; the

---

20 Cf. Heinz Timmermann, Die Beziehungen EU-Rußland, Berichte des Bundesinstituts für ostwissenschaftliche und internationale Studien, No. 60, Cologne 1994.

European Parliament has so far postponed its approval until the conflict is settled.

The PCA with the Ukraine has not yet entered into force but reflects the Union's interest in the economic and political viability of this important country. In terms of technical assistance the TACIS programme (standing for 'technical assistance to the CIS') has acquired the same importance as the PHARE programme for the Central and Eastern European countries: a wide-ranging series of projects to restructure state enterprises, promote private sector development, agricultural reform, etc. In the last three years over 500 m ECU were given to Russia in connection with this programme.

This no doubt incomplete overview demonstrates the European Union's long-term strategy vis-à-vis the former communist camp. It is a strategy of wide-ranging assistance and cooperation. But it is, no less important, linked to a set of political conditions adjusted to the situation of each country, to its needs and capability for reform. Seen in this light, the various association and partnership agreements with the former communist countries are a formidable, if indirect instrument in the European Union's still meagre arsenal of foreign policy. To be effective, it demands a high degree of consensus and concertation amongst the Union's members: it is here where policies and practices jointly acquired over the years, can be put to use; it is here also where the Commission, with its staff, can assume fully its responsibility as coordinator of and watchdog over the implementation of a common policy.

From 'East' to 'South'

In sum, then, the European Union is set to weave a widening web of new ties and commitments with what we loosely called its 'Eastern periphery'. Such enlargement eastwards, however welcome, if not inevitable, calls for compensations or complementation in the South. The Latin members of the Union point out, not without justification, that the Mediterranean is as important to the Union as is Central and Eastern Europe. The reasons for this importance may be different, but they are hardly less relevant. The Union must therefore mobilize additional resources to address them. And it must do so in a more coherent and substantiated way than so far. To be sure, some agreements existed between Brussels and countries like Turkey or Morocco: Cyprus and Malta are waiting in the *anti-chambre* for admission. And so in fact does Turkey with whom, almost as a consolation price, a customs union is ready to enter into force. But bilateral relations are no substitute for a comprehensive and future-oriented strategic concept.

In mid-October 1994 the time for such a more comprehensive concept had come. The European Commission put forward a proposal for an 'economic and security pact' with countries of the Middle East and North Africa. It points out the growing gap between the 'rich' and the 'poor' countries of the region, the threat of what is all too loosely called 'Islamic fundamentalism' and the possibility of mass migration. In order to deal with these potential risks the Commission proposes the creation of a large free-trade zone. Furthermore, it calls for a doubling of aid to the region over the next five years. Financial assistance to the Mediterranean area will be increased to 4,685 bn ECUs for the period of 1997–2001. The convocation of a peace and security conference – possibly along the model of CSCE – is envisaged.

This is a highly ambitious project. It would involve the Union in the Mediterranean to an extent and with consequences that go well beyond anything it has done so far anywhere. The Union, by force of necessity but also in order to balance an otherwise too 'eastern-oriented' engagement, is entering here a *terra incognita* with multiple political and security implications. It is likely to draw the Union into what the Americans call a 'new ball game'. Here, no less than in Europe's eastern frontier, it will find itself slowly but inevitably drawn into fields and on issues for which it has to develop, conceptually and institutionally, the corresponding policy and the instruments to carry it out.

So far, this policy is piece-meal. It probably cannot be otherwise, given both the novelty of the Union's environment and of the tasks that go with it. To date, we can distinguish three levels of intensity of commitment: in Central and Eastern Europe it carries clearly a political dimension, first, by linking economic cooperation with political consolidation, and, second, by making it understood that association today may lead to integration tomorrow. Russia and, most likely Ukraine and, to a lesser degree, the other CIS countries, find themselves in a different category. Here the emphasis is on as constructive a co-operation as possible: partnership surely, but no membership would seem to be the name of the game. The third and again different tier is formed by the ill-defined and heterogeneous group of Mediterranean countries. Here again we have the full range from promise of membership to loose association. On the more distant horizon, we may even see emerge a system of political cooperation between the North and the South Mediterranean.

These differentiations are, of course, no accident. They are as inevitable as they are significative. For at least two reasons. First, because they clearly lay open the limitations of what a Union whose primary objective is still economic can do politically. Second, because the widening net of external commitments is, by necessity and changing circumstances, almost bound to acquire an ever greater political weight and thrust. And, third, because member countries may (and in fact do) have different interests and priorities when it comes to deciding which region, Eastern or Southern Europe, North or South, should be offered how much and on what conditions. Inevitably, such divergencies are bound to introduce occasional tensions or animosities. They are bound to grow if and when new members are admitted, most of them net receivers, and the Union's budget will be curtailed. It is here probably more than anywhere else that the cohesion of the Union and the solidarity of its members will be put to a serious test.

Versus 'global engagement'

This brings us to what we call the geographical 'outer circle' of the Union's foreign relations. There is, of course, the 'special relationship' with Japan and the emerging and increasingly dense network of relations with the states in the South Pacific. Most of them are now members of the ASEAN (Association of South East Asian Nations) with which a formal link was established in November 1978. Three other regions deserve, however, to be mentioned more specifically: the first because of its strategic and political priority, the second because of its geographic proximity and conflict potential, and the third because of its cultural affinity, all three because they are, each in its own way, of great economic importance to Europe.

The first is obviously the United States, at the same time ally and competitor of Western Europe. Together with Canada it is tied to this Europe through numerous institutions – the Atlantic Alliance being the political backbone of this relationship. It is more than a marriage of convenience: strategically indispensable during the Cold War, and politically still essential today, there are now efforts to broaden it into other fields of common interest. The Transatlantic Declaration, signed between the Union and the United States (plus Canada) in November 1990, points into that direction.[21] No doubt prompted by the then escalating crisis in the Gulf and growing uncertainties about developments in the Soviet Union, it is not just a confirmation of a long-standing and close partnership. It contains also a recognition of the Union's growing weight in world affairs. From it flows a whole series of commitments which the Union will have to honour in the future. Whether it can do so without at the same time broadening its own policy-making capacity, remains to be seen. Clearly, transatlantic relations require a new and more comprehensive approach lest they slip down the dangerous slope towards fierce economic competition and an ever weaker political solidarity.

Proposals for the creation of a transatlantic economic space have been aired for some time. They were taken up again by the Commission in Summer 1995. With more than a dozen bilateral agreements in the East there are indeed good reasons to balance these with something equivalent with the Union's most important partner in the West, the United States. More important, however, is the recognition that the United States and the European Union, the latter even as a yet 'incomplete' political power, are today the most influential actors on the world scene. As such they share common responsibilities but may also

---

21 See the German text of the 'Common declaration on the relations between the European Community and the United States', November 23, 1990, in: Europa-Archiv, 1(1991), pp. D 18–21.

develop ever more diverging interests. Having lost their common adversary, the Soviet Union, they feel freer to become economically more competitive, even at the risk of greater political tension. Both may therefore feel the need to tie their expanding but more vulnerable relations to a set of common rules, be it in form of a full-fledged treaty, of various sectoral agreements or even of a genuine and broadly gaged pact. Views on the necessity or even feasibility of such a strengthening of transatlantic relations diverge. It would seem that this time Europeans are pushing and Americans hesitating. The latter fear that protracted negotiations without Europeans, still far from speaking with one voice, may bring into the open more diverging than converging interests. At the same time, the United States sees itself in the centre of international economy with interests and commitments now as much in the West, i.e. the Pacific, as in the East, i.e. Europe. It is geopolitics applied to economics and trade – a strategy whose importance the European Union has not yet fully grasped when it comes to defining its own geopolitical position in the world of tomorrow.

The second region the Union wants to expand its commitments to is the Middle East. There is, based on various agreements (1964, 1970 and 1975), a long-standing relationship with Israel. The Union proposes to expand it, both in substance and by concluding agreements with Morocco and Tunisia. Negotiations pursuing a similar aim with Egypt and other Mediterranean countries are envisaged. A 'triangular relationship' between the Union, the Mashrik countries (Egypt, Syria, Lebanon) and Israel point to what the European Council, at its summit in Essen in December 1994, called a 'Euro-Mediterranean partnership' that includes the Middle East. With the Gulf Cooperation Council, consisting of the six Arab countries in the Gulf, the Union has already a formal though rather loose relationship. In its communication on 'Future Relations and Cooperation between the Community and the Middle East'[22], the Commission mentions not only the desirability of closer relations with the Middle Eastern countries. It also stresses that these relations "should be based on respect for human rights and the

---

22 Cf. Commission of the European Communities, Future Relations and Cooperation Between the Community and the Middle East, Brussels, 8 September 1993.

strengthening of democracy": a clear reference to, and insistence on, the conditionality that we find ever more consistently mentioned in all present or proposed agreements.

To a certain extent this is also the case with regard to the Union's relations with Latin America.[23] A number of bilateral and preferential agreements exist already (e.g. with Andean and Central American countries). A major step towards a broader, bi-regional association between the Union and Latin America was taken in 1994. On October 31st of that year, the Council of Ministers approved a 14-point 'Basic Document on the Relations of the European Union with Latin America and the Caribbean'[24]. It reaffirmed the Union's commitment to such a broader relationship. Six weeks later, at its December summit in Essen, the Council called on the Commission to prepare for negotiations with MERCOSUR on a trade liberalization agreement. In February 1995 closer links with Mexico through an economic partnership were proposed.[25]

Such an opening of Europe to Latin America does not come as a surprise. It shows, first, the latter's growing economic weight; second, its willingness to diversify its trade relations traditionally too exclusively oriented towards, if not too dependent on, the United States. MERCOSUR is probably the most promising attempt at sub-regional economic cooperation, if not integration in Latin America (there are six others). With Brazil, Argentina, Uruguay and Paraguay as its members it would seem the right address to get the Union's opening towards that continent off the ground. Given the political fluidity of South American politics, with regimes of often doubtful democratic and human rights credentials, the Union is faced here with a particularly delicate task when it comes to insisting on the kind of conditionality that it applies to other parts of the world. Still, in its document mentioned above, the Union does "pay tribute to and support the endeavours undertaken in the region (i.e. Latin America and the Caribbean)

---

23 Cf. Table VII a and VII b in the annex.
24 Cf. Europe and Latin America: A Partnership for Action, Basic Document on the Relations of the European Union with Latin America and the Caribbean, Luxembourg, 31 October 1994.
25 Cf. The New Europe and its Impact on Latin America, Dossier No. 53 prepared by the Institute for European-Latin American Relations, Madrid, March 1995.

to consolidate representative democracy and the Rule of Law". The document furthermore contains a whole of desiderata in various fields that the Union wishes to be taken into account by its Latin American partners. How much pressure it is prepared to use for the sake of their implementation will be a tough test for the credibility of the Union's policy of conditionality. This is, thankfully, a problem it does not have with the remaining EFTA countries, Norway and Switzerland, Iceland and Liechtenstein.

This overview does not show the full panoply of the Union's instruments through and with which it can defend its interests, use its economic leverage and influence the world that surrounds it. The arsenal is, of course, much richer as it befits a community of now fifteen mostly highly industrialized and wealthy states. The Union today has at its disposal diplomatic missions, representatives and information offices all over the world; in turn, some one hundred states entertain missions in Brussels, accredited with the Union and its Commission. The President of the Commission takes part in meetings of the G-7, the group of the seven major industrialized countries as well as in the summit conferences of the OSCE.

Taken together, the agreements referred to before make for an impressive list. They form a network of global dimension. As such they do not simply reflect the European Union's involvement in the world economy but also the degree of responsibility – economic, political, social and ecological – that goes with them. Whether these instruments are sufficient, always adequate and properly handled, is open to debate. Abuse and corruption are almost fatally present when millions of ECUs flow in all directions and occasionally without sufficient control. Aid to developing countries was – and still is – being squandered by both donors and recipients. There is no reason to assume why this should be different with as generous a donor as the European Union and its Commission.

Still, on balance, one can say that no other international institution has as wide and diverse a network of agreements as the Union. It represents a powerful tool, used for the economic and social benefit of all sides. Whether this can be translated into anything more – such as crisis prevention or conflict management – has yet to be proven. As long as this is uncertain, we must conclude that the Union, with all its impressive arsenal, is still no political power in the traditional sense. Perhaps, it may never want to be one.

Towards more politics

Whether it likes it or not: the European Union after the Cold War finds itself surrounded by a totally different environment. There are no clear borders or 'fronts' anymore. The world – and with it the Union – is in a period of transition or 'interlude'.[26] Here, new priorities and new rules of the game have to be developed. The players are still jockeying for positions and pursuing often conflicting interests.

To all this, the Union will have to adjust. And yet, in this setting of almost total fluidity it is, by all accounts and standards, an exception. It is the most integrated and institutionalized international body in the world. It has withstood, not without some damage to its internal cohesion and queries about its future, the waves of change that swept Europe after the fall of the Berlin wall. The price for such survival is that it finds itself confronted with an ever-growing number of demands, expectations and responsibilities on all sides and levels. Most of them are of the kind that cannot simply be met and satisfied by trade or aid, finance or assistance. In short: the panoply of instruments that the Union has developed and applied so impressively in the four decades of its existence cries out for enlargement.

The need for a CFSP, so often invoked and so often ignored, is now recognized by many inside and outside the Union. However, there is still a big gap between recognition of a necessity and acting on it. Our overview of the Union's instruments of power shows therefore at least three things:

First, the weight and influence of the Union in international affairs is largely a function of its economic power. Most of its external relations are either of an exclusively economic nature or have an important economic content. Given the history and objectives of the Union, this

26 Cf. Werner Weidenfeld, Ernstfall Europa, in: Internationale Politik 1(1995), pp. 11–19.

does not come as a surprise. It merely shows the inevitable limitation which even an institution like the Union has either to accept or to overcome if and when it is expected to take on new, more ambitious and wider tasks.

Second, the Community has used the various means at its disposal in a generally constructive way. Agreements such as the treaties of association or the Lomé Conventions have inevitably a political connotation. It may be implicit or indirect. But it is important nevertheless. To stabilize a given country by offering economic assistance, credits and advantageous terms of trade, is as much a political act as is the conclusion of a treaty on the recognition of borders. Beyond that, the Community has moved either openly or surrepetitiously into the political realm by making its economic assistance dependent on political conditions. With the waning of the East-West conflict it could do so better and more outspokenly. The West's linking of economic stability to modicum of political correctness could now become more pronounced. In this sense, if in no other, the European Union is assuming a political responsibility that only a few years ago it would have been reluctant to assume.

Third and following from the preceding, the European Union is realizing that even in a world in which economics have become so preponderant, politics remain the backbone of international order and national self-esteem. From this follows the logical conclusion that the Union, too, will not be able to make use of the full economic potential and play the role it is expected to play in the new international environment if it does not enlarge the gamut of its instruments of power. It would be sad indeed if, by failing to do that, it would fall in line with all those institutions that after the Cold War have either become obsolete or are unable to move beyond mere cosmetic reforms. However transitional the present period may be, we can be sure that it will be a harsh judge for those political institutions whose only motive is to survive rather than to serve.

IV. More Vulnerabilities

This seems to be a strange title. What can 'new vulnerabilities' be in an era that is thought to have left all the vulnerabilities and threats of war and nuclear holocaust behind? It is indeed true that the danger of an international war has receded into the background worldwide and surely also on the European continent after the double end of the Cold War and of the Soviet Union as one of its principal instigators. It is also true that various real or imagined threats have either disappeared or do not haunt any longer the politicians and their bureaucracies – be it the spectre of another oil embargo or of a shortage of vital raw materials. The ideological barriers to dialogue and the political inhibitions to cooperate almost totally evaporated in this high-spirited climate of general *détente*. With very few exceptions, everybody is now free to deal with everybody. This allows for a globalization of the economy and of political intercourse limited only by the finiteness of the globe. 'Anything goes' as a distinguished German journalist formulated it when describing his country's all-round foreign policy.[27]

Waning influence

It is perhaps precisely this possibility for omnipresence and 'free for all' which could generate a new kind of vulnerability. Europe is far from immune to it. There is, first and most obviously, an increasingly fierce

27 Cf. Josef Joffe, Deutsche Außenpolitik – postmodern, in: Internationale Politik 1(1995), p. 45.

economic competition. The catchword here is the quasi new phenomenon of 'emerging markets'. To them belong mainly Asian countries. They are seen as becoming a growing challenge to Europe and its economy and, possibly still more serious, its political and social traditions. Europe's concept of liberal democracy on the one hand, and its deeply engrained commitment to the *état providence*, the welfare state, on the other, are now confronted with concepts and habits which are, if not diametrically opposed to, then certainly very different from them. Asian societies, we are told,[28] place much more emphasis on the role of the family and family traditions, on hard work and discipline, on political obedience and economic performance than do those in Western Europe. Unlike Europe, Asia is described as politically stable, demographically stronger and physically younger. The shift of influence and affluence from the West to the East would thus appear to be almost preordained when politics matter less and economics ever more. We would move towards a world in which oversold democratic values and human rights, while no doubt important, have less relevance as Europe (together with North America) no longer sets the tone and the direction for mankind.

Such juxtaposition is oversimplified. It leaves out many facets in both East and West. It does not pay sufficient attention to continents as important as Latin America or as problem-ridden as Africa. It nevertheless points to a fundamental change in international politics and the way states and societies see their role in this newly emerging world. The end of the Cold War brought with it also the erstwhile end of the last totalitarian ideology – communism. Of all the ideologies that were born in the 19th and put into practice in the 20th century – from fascism via national-socialism to communism – the last one was the most costly socio-political experiment mankind ever experienced. It was total in its ambition to control man, society and state, and global in its strategic dimension. But, with its European roots, it posed an alternative to Western liberal democracy, no less rooted in European political thinking. In this sense, if in no other, the confrontation and

28 Cf. Tommy Koh, The 10 Values that undergird East Asian Strength and Success, in: International Herald Tribune, 11/12 December 1993.

competition between these two concepts were a 'European-Western' one but carried out on a global scale. It was a struggle about the position and rights of man in society and vis-à-vis the state, with both sides presenting themselves as the true defenders of the less European-inspired ideal and promotion of human rights.

The end of the communist experience does certainly not signal the end of history, leaving the Western political credo as the only remaining and thus prevailing one. On the contrary: it would seem that now, at long last, ideas, traditions and policies of other, non-Western societies can come to the fore, be they Asian, African or Islamic. Encouraged and spurred by their economic performance, particularly Asian countries make it clear that their own system and culture are different from those of the West but no less valid and effective. Emboldened by their often staggering economic growth many Asian nations – like Singapore or Malaysia, Indonesia or, most visibly, China – feel strong enough to challenge this very West when it comes to such highly politicized questions like human rights or democratization of their political regime. This is not a "clash of civilizations" (to use Huntington's much quoted phrase). But it may announce what a Singaporean diplomat anticipates becoming a "struggle between an Atlantic impulse and a Pacific impulse"[29]. A complex issue, if there ever was one. It is mentioned here because it lays open two important facts. First, it shows that the 'Europeanization' of the world – a result of Europe's colonialism and political and economic preponderance over centuries – has come to an end. Europe and its American off-spring, the United States, will no doubt remain important actors in the world. But Europe, whether fragmented or ever more integrated, will be confronted with other actors of no less status and self-confidence. This 'other world' will defend different ways of life and different concepts of man, society and state. It may have a different understanding of the meaning of power and the role of armed force both at home and abroad. The international community will thus be more pluralistic and competitive; economic power and technological innovation may become more important than military strength or an elaborate system of social security.

---

29 Kishore Mahbubani, The Pacific Impulse, in: Survival, No. 1, Vol. 37 (Spring 1995), p. 105.

In this new environment of globalized competition Europe is discovering its own economic vulnerability. Its social and political stability was very much a function of its economic growth and the belief in its indefinite continuation. Of course, neither was, nor ever will be, assured. But as long as progress in integration was equated with progress in growth, the European Community found few detractors and many supporters. This changed the moment growth became less certain and integration, for political reasons, less inescapable. In other words, the cost-benefit ratio between sacrifices for more integration and hopes for more economic returns as its result, seems to be shifting against the latter. The European Commission, rarely beloved but grudgingly accepted, comes under increasing fire. Its huge bureaucracy, its multilayered system of rules and regulations, of protectionism and subsidies, are easy targets for criticism in a climate in which such criticism is no longer seen as disloyalty to the 'European cause'. Doubts are now common fare as to whether this huge European edifice, both conceptually and physically, is not too cumbersome to remain competitive, and not too tradition-loaded to be innovative.

As the awareness of economic vulnerability grows in Europe, so does the willingness of reducing it by overhauling many time-honoured structures and policies in the member countries and in the Union itself. European integration has always progressed when faced with challenges coming from the outside. The first came from the Soviet colossus in the fifties and sixties, the second from the American superiority in the seventies, and the third from Japanese efficiency in the eighties. Who knows whether it will not come from the emerging markets of Asia in the nineties, and from China or India in the next millennium? Seen in this light, vulnerability can also have its positive effect: as a stimulus for overhauling the process of European integration and adapting it to a new and more demanding international environment.

Transnational challenges

The second kind of vulnerability is different. But it, too, is linked to what we called the process of globalization. It stems from the emergence of a new kind of transnational actors – mostly national in origin but often international in impact. This phenomenon is not new. It began in earnest when economic and political barriers went down as they did in the 1960s and 1970s. Even under the rather inhospitable conditions of the Cold War ever more institutions, organizations and enterprises made the world their home and their place of action. Helped by an ever greater mobility and a network of ever more accessible systems of communication these non-state actors became the very symbols of what people today call 'globalization'. Thus the number of multinational companies has increased from 7,000 in 1970 to over 37,000 in 1995. Drug cartels operate worldwide, and so do banks and stock exchanges. International financial transactions amount to one trillion dollars per day. More often than not they happen with little or no control on part of governments. All these and many other developments affect simultaneously and instantly the life of millions of people. They do so mostly in a peaceful though no less important way than did wars in previous times.

Indeed, it would seem that the use of armed force has shifted from the international to the national stage. Of the 82 wars fought in the years 1993/94 only three were conducted between two or more states. All the others were – some of them still are – internal conflicts of various kinds. They are, as witnesses the tribal war in Somalia, the butchery in Rwanda and the civil war in former Yugoslavia, no less bloody and senseless.[30] It is as yet premature to conclude from this that the world is becoming more peaceful internationally and more conflictual internally, or that man's innate aggressiveness is, for lack of an external aggressor, turning against his own society and neighbour.

These are new developments, if not by their very nature then by their international, if not global dimension. Together, they are difficult to seize in their manifold ramifications. But all of them point to challenges

---

30 Cf. Hans Magnus Enzensberger, Aussichten auf den Bürgerkrieg, Frankfurt 1994.

which states have to face and deal with. Some of them escape the control of governments, others affect the lifestyle or well-being of entire communities. That, for instance, is the case with the as yet uncontrolled proliferation of light weapons. Their easy availability and their abundance allow private gangs to fight wars against each other or terrorize the official forces of order. That is the case of the international drug traffic whose annual turnover is estimated to be some 300 bn dollars. The economy of entire countries has become dependent on the production, processing and trading of drugs. Much, if not most of them find their way to the industrialized countries, North America and Europe in the first place.[31]

Pessimists may see in this unusual onslaught new and serious sources of vulnerability against which there are few or only insufficient remedies. Optimists, on the other hand, may see in them precisely the kind of 'enemy' that Europe needs to continue its march towards closer cooperation and integration. Their argument is that only in this way Europe will be capable of coping with the problems that are no longer confined to individual states and therefore demand an international and surely, first of all, a European response.

Uncertainties in the East

The third vulnerability is again of a different kind. It has to do, on the one hand, with the uncertain future of Russia and its periphery, i.e. the other members of the CIS. On the other hand, it relates to the 'build-down' of American military presence and political engagement on the continent. The two issues are linked to, or, better perhaps, contingent upon each other. A full withdrawal of the United States from Europe would give greater weight to Russia, even in its present dire state; a consolidation of Russia's economy at home and a reaffirmation of its dominance in the CIS, would in all likelihood meet with an American response.

---

31 Cf. Observatoire géopolitique des drogues, Etat des drogues, drogues des Etats, Paris 1994; Ramses 95: Synthèse annuelle de l'actualité mondiale, sous la direction de Thierry de Montbrial et Pierre Jacquet, Paris 1994, pp. 44–46.

In both cases, Europe, or the European Union, would find itself in the middle. Of course, there is the Atlantic Alliance and there are projects to reinforce transatlantic relations. Of course, Europe has a special interest in tying Russia into a network of agreements such as the above mentioned Partnership and Cooperation Agreements concluded with the European Union. The members of the latter have armed forces sufficiently strong to justify a substantial reduction of American forces now that the Soviet Union and the Warsaw Pact do not exist anymore. But they are in their present state hardly strong enough to stand up to a reinvigorated and expanding Russia which still has an arsenal of several thousand nuclear warheads.

This kind of European vulnerability is old and new at the same time. As table VIII in the annex shows, the Union maintains more conventional forces than the United States; its two million men correspond roughly to what Russia's delapidated and humiliated army can presently muster. But this impressive figure is misleading. It represents little else than the addition of the armed forces of the fifteen member states. It is in other words a highly heterogeneous accumulation of armies with rarely standardized weaponry and little, if any interoperability, guided by different security interests and different concepts of strategy.

The Western European Union expected to become the nucleus of a European defence force, is still hardly more than a 'sleeping beauty' when it comes to command and control of armed force. To be sure, its membership has grown. But it did so less in number than in various categories of members. Nobody dares to think of what might happen if a serious conflict in Europe would break out and reveal that the 'beauty' has no arms. This may change in the future if and when WEU member states succeed in putting military units under WEU command. Whether and when they will be willing to do so, depends critically on the European Union's progress towards greater political cohesion.

In the meantime, Eurocorps is making some headway. With its original nucleus of a German-French brigade it was expanded into a corps whose tasks were defined by a German-French declaration in May 1992. It was further elaborated in the 'Petersberg Declaration' of the

WEU in June 1992. Both Belgium and later Spain pledged to put a brigade at the corps' disposal. The Eurocorps is expected to operate within the framework of both NATO and the WEU. Once more, we are faced with a compromise. It confirms that Europeans are still torn between their allegiance to NATO (and the United States) and their intention to progress towards a more independent European defence organization of their own.[32]

To these glaring institutional and conceptual weaknesses has to be added yet another. Europe is suffering from a new kind of vulnerability in the sense that it now embraces a much larger group of like-minded countries most of which wish to join the Union. The original nucleus of six and then twelve European states was, with the exception of Ireland, identical with the Atlantic Alliance's European wing. It is no longer. The Union and the Alliance are open to accept new members or to offer to non-members assistance and cooperation (the first in form of special agreements, the second in form of Partnership for Peace Programmes).

With Austria, Finland and Sweden the Union has admitted three formally still neutral or non-aligned countries. It is thus moving east- and northwards. In so doing it is taking on new responsibilities to- wards a region that has the legitimate right to consider itself as part of a now enlarged Europe. At the same time Western Europe could become the hostage of such expansion without integration. It has built so far a halfway house. It offers, as mentioned before, help and the prospect of later membership with either the European Union or NATO, or even both, but without offering also the defence and se- curity that should go with it. It lays itself open to situations of conflict or unrest between or within one or the other of the Central and East European countries without having as yet the means to deal with them adequately.

In a stable and peaceful Europe, supported by a cooperative and democratically constituted Russia, such contingencies may, it is hoped, never arise. And yet, the possibility that they will, cannot be totally

---

32 On the Eurocorps see, Bundesministerium der Verteidigung, Weißbuch 1994 (also in English), Bonn 1994; and La Documentation française. Livre blanc sur la Défense 1994, Paris 1994.

discounted. In such a case both the Union and the Alliance are doubly vulnerable: to the accusation of not having been able to prevent the conflict, and to the suspicion of never really having been serious about offering such protection in the first place.

Losing momentum

The fourth vulnerability has to do with the European Union's own future – or rather the uncertainty about the kind of future the Union is going to have. In a first go, such assertion may sound enigmatic. We mean by this the following. The Treaty of Maastricht, praised and vilified at the same time, is supposed to outline the future course and destiny of European integration. It invites member states to what, in American terminology, is called a 'building-bloc approach'. This means a logical and step-by-step progress towards a pre-set goal. In our case this goal is a politically and institutionally coherent entity of an as yet unspecified number of member countries. Economic union and monetary union – however defined – would be given priority over a political union whose exact contours will have to be defined more precisely. Still, the Union treaty is meant to set in motion a movement towards an ever more and more closely integrated unity. As such, the treaty with its final fore-ordained destination is a useful device – in theory. Alas, we all by now know how difficult, if not nearly impossible it is to realize it in practice.

The horizons of Europe's future are set high indeed. To attain them at a given but no doubt still distant date, requires the mobilization and concertation of all available forces. It will no less call for an ambitious programme of internal re-organization and streamlining as well as the continued adjustment of the Union to a rapidly changing and demanding environment. Expectations as to what the Union can, or will, achieve on these three fronts are being scaled down as the row of years of unfulfilled pledges grows. Expectations were probably too high at any time. This is surely true when we look at the numerous applicants for admission. They, more than the 'insiders', see in the Union the main-stay of Europe's order of tomorrow. Such a perspective, whether

83

false or true, would indeed suggest that the Union has become the victim of its own success. Ironically, if not sadly, this became clear the very moment the initial impetus for further integration had already begun to wane. It happened at almost the same time as the East-West confrontation was running its course and nearing its end. The tremendous effort of achieving the single market – and in fact its very creation – had sapped a great amount of energy; the intense and difficult negotiations for the Maastricht Treaty and the no less demanding process of its ratification by the member states (including two popular referenda in Denmark first, and in France afterwards) apparently absorbed whatever energy and incentive were left. Instead, ever more questions were raised about the implementation of the treaty stipulations and objectives and about the *finalité* and eventual goal of the integration process as such.

This *finalité*, the eventual objective of European integration, may undergo some alterations in the future when it comes to defining the precise forms and extent of integration. The latter is a term open to many interpretations. Whether, in the end, the European Union will be more like a federal state, a confederation or a union *sui generis*, matters less than the fact that its final form should be irreversible and that its supreme objective – peace and freedom in and for Europe – must remain intact. Indeed, the fact that European statesmen want to make this unified Europe irreversible stems from their fear, not quite unfounded, that "Europe's past might still triumph over Europe's future",[33] that Europe might again disintegrate into rivalling fractions and senseless power games. It would then have lost – perhaps forever – the chance of creating the kind of peace order that its founders dreamt of after the war.

---

33 Cf. Michael Stürmer, Die Revanche der Geschichte – Welt im Umbruch, in: Politische Studien 331 (September/October 1993), p. 14.

New priorities

For Western Europe at least the first priority therefore can no longer be simply to get still richer and secure its own well-being. Both objectives are now secondary to the one of becoming more efficient in preventing a recurrence of nationalist egotism within the Union, and consolidate its wider European environment outside. Such double *finalité* is, needless to say, still more difficult to attain than the previous one: first, because there will be many more parties involved – members, future members, associates and outsiders; second, because the Union will have to function, and survive, in a many more fluid international environment which lessens the sense of common purpose and invites the affirmation of more narrow national, if not nationalistic interests.

No doubt, the end of the Cold War played a role in all this: for once not an entirely positive one. Having achieved much of its goals – keeping peace in (Western) Europe, promoting economic recovery and prosperity, and fending off the Soviet-communist challenge – it seemed only natural that countries, governments and people began to compare the costs of further integration with those of simply sticking to the *status quo* attained so far. The fact that the end of the Cold War made it at long last possible that both neutral and former communist countries can now join the Union, did little to discredit such a conclusion. Pragmatism began to prevail over whatever modest idealism was still alive.

A 'yes' to accepting new members is not equivalent to a 'yes' to further integration; the fourth enlargement (with Austria, Finland and Sweden) has yet to be followed by more than cosmetic internal reform. Whether such reforms will go beyond the inevitable institutional streamlining remains to be seen. If the pressure for more substantive integration does not come from inside, i.e. the present members, one can wonder whether it will come again from outside. It goes without saying that any initiative in this respect coming from within the Union would be infinitely healthier and more enduring in its effects than pressure coming from outside.

Integration cannot live and last without the free consensus of the 'integrated members'. To be sure, external events have influenced, and often accelerated the creation of practically all federations and confederations. This was true for the Swiss confederation as it was for the United States, for the German Bund and for the European Community. But none of these unions could hold together without the determination of its members to stay and progress together, to adjust their common, originally fragile institutions to the changing internal needs and to a changing environment. Where this is not done the union's cohesion begins to loosen. Centrifugal forces will resuscitate and parochial lobbies will raise their heads. The elaborate tissue of the Union may then disintegrate. As a consequence, its common position towards the outside will lose persuasiveness and impact. Under such circumstances the Union might become more exposed to outside influence or pressure. It could become vulnerable because less resilient in its capacity to act in unison and to pursue a policy sustained by all its members.

At the end of this overview of new vulnerabilities we must ask whether the Union in its present state and with a future chartered by the Maastricht Treaty is capable of handling and overcoming whatever vulnerability it may be exposed to. The answer is probably no. It is still far from having developed the kind of foreign and security policy that could compensate for a further withdrawal of the United States or meet the challenge of a newly constituted and enlarged Russia. It has not yet fully implemented and expanded the Schengen agreement on the free flow of internal migration and the control of immigration. Issues like drug trafficking and organized crime call for more sustained efforts of cooperation, if not integration. Most seriously of all, we can observe a loosening of the Union's cohesion, a receding willingness to push for far-reaching internal reform and possibly even for maintaining the entire *acquis communautaire*.

Thus, main questions remain: about the necessity or feasibility of a monetary union, about the further progress towards political union, about Europe's defence identity and its capability to move towards greater independence in its own defence and security policy. Do we know whether the political union, if it comes to pass, will be anywhere close to the one the early federalists dreamed? Can we even be sure whether it will resemble the union envisaged by the Maastricht Treaty?

Put very starkly: the European Union in its present phase of uncertainty, combined with the prospect of further enlargement, risks becoming its own worst enemy. It is feeding doubts about its own *finalité*, its own final destination as the central political actor on the European continent and a major player on the international stage. Such self-doubt is perhaps the greatest vulnerability of all. Little would it matter how many members such a union can eventually boast of. If it does not believe in its own future it will hardly develop further into the kind of forward-moving force that Europe needs and the world expects.

V. New Centres of Concern

At the beginning of this study we described what we call the changing landscape in which the European Union finds itself today – and will have to live with tomorrow. It will have to act on, and react to, issues as diverse as the human rights situation in Rwanda and the future of the textile industry in Poland. It will be expected to present a common stand in the new World Trade Organization and on the future of Bosnia. In brief: the world and its innumerable issues and institutions are waiting for a 'European policy' – and the latter will have to answer the call.

With hindsight, the Cold War with the structures and rules it imposed on the international community, looks fairly orderly. The European Community grew and developed in this divided world which this 'war' created. There was never any doubt that the Community belonged to the West. Departing from its original vision of becoming a pan-European federation, it had to content itself with an important but clearly circumscribed part of Western Europe. It knew its place both as the continental foothold of the Atlantic Alliance and the bulwark against the Soviet bloc. Both missions helped to generate internal cohesion and to elaborate common external positions. Not that either was always easy: an inflated nostalgia for these 'good old times' is misplaced. Still, the Community, as it developed and enlarged, had a sense of orientation and was confident about its future. To be sure, it had its concerns. Some of them were serious. There was the Gaullist challenge in the sixties, the oil embargo in the seventies, and the missile crisis in the eighties.

Acting globally

The end of the East-West confrontation changed many of these givens. Old concerns disappeared together with the iron curtain and the Soviet Union. New concerns emerged as the continent grew together again and the world became an open stage for economic rather than ideo-logical rivalry, hardly constrained by fear of political reprisals emanat-ing from whatever dominating power is left. The first and foremost new concern for the Union is therefore that of learning to think and act globally. Not just Europe but the world in its new and less con-stricted configuration has become wider. It demands more attention. The Union is now expected to review its relations with North America and other OECD countries like Japan and Australia. It has pledged to play a constructive role in the peace process slowly and often painfully engaged between Israel and the Palestinians. It must build bridges to, and compete with, the newly emerging markets of Latin America, South East Asia and the Far East. At the same time it must preserve its commitments to the nearly seventy member countries of the Lomé convention, particularly to the very weak ones in Black Africa. And it cannot remain indifferent to the present or impending political and social turbulences in the Gulf region on whose oil it still vitally de-pends.

Beyond this more 'classic' country and region approach, the Union will have to review and promote its activities in, and commitments to, a multitude of international institutions: from GATT to the WTO, from the OSCE to NATO, from cooperation with regional organiza-tions such as the Gulf Cooperation Council and the Association of South East Asian Nations, with the North American Free Trade Area and the Association of Pacific Economic Cooperation. The Union will also have to take position if and when it comes to a reform of the United Nations and, above all, its Security Council. Here, two of its members, France and Britain, belong to the privileged group of the five permanent members. Germany and Italy do not – nor indeed do coun-tries like Japan or India. Should the Union not plead for a single seat, representing its fifteen members rather than be – only partly and occa-sionally – represented by just two? Unrealistic (and, as far as the two current holders of the seats are concerned, undesirable) as such suggestion would seem to be at the moment, such a merger would provide a welcome stimulus for the Union's formulation of a common policy when it comes to important UN-related issues.

In a similar vein, the G-7 (with, as its members, the United States, Canada, France, Britain, Germany, Japan and Italy, and, as a half-outsider, Russia when it comes to dealing with political-strategic matters) is in need of overhaul. It, too, should have a more equitable representation (Asia, for instance, is represented only by Japan). Again, the Union will have to declare its position and make suggestions as to its own role and representation. The Bretton Woods institutions – the World Bank and the International Monetary Fund – are in many ways either obsolete or in need of profound reform. To be sure, no such reform is possible without an active involvement of the United States. But the time is over when all initiatives were expected to come – and in fact usually did – from Washington. Given its financial weight and its farreaching aid programmes it would be anything but natural if the Union in consultation with other major donors, would push for an institutional rejuvenation and political re-orientation of these two venerable institutions.

Finally, as more and more issues grow into those of global concern – demographic explosion, mass migration and environmental degradation being amongst them – they, too, call for a more concerted handling. Here, the Union could act as a pioneer by showing how such issues are being addressed, and actually coped with, at a regional level. The Schengen agreement on free circulation amongst several member states, however incomplete, can serve as one example; it is hoped that a Europe-wide cooperation of police forces (Europol) may soon become another. Together they show, however, that partial integration or cooperation can often create more problems instead of solving them: a Europe of different speeds or with different degrees of integration is far from being an ideal solution. It may be inevitable on a continent as heterogeneous as Europe but it should not be accepted as final.

Thinking and acting globally will – or at least should – have a unifying effect on the Union and the way it sees and defines its own role. In a certain way, it finds itself in a situation similar to that in which it had to define its response to, first, the Soviet military dominance, then to American technological superiority and, finally, to Japanese economic competition. While different in nature and intensity, there were challenges from the outside the European Community had to react to. The difference between them and those of today is, however, twofold. First, being general in nature and lying more in the future than in the present, the global challenges are much more difficult to identify. They do not come from a specific country or region. They come from everywhere and nowhere. They are hazy in their contours and uncertain in their effects. Hence, they may not, or not yet, be perceived as real and imminent threats and thus call for concerted and concrete action. All indications, however, are that before long they will become real. And they will then possibly be more serious and more lasting than the previous ones.[34]

The second difference follows from the first. The Union now 'on the loose' in a largely unstructured world, will have to develop more consciously its own political identity. It will have to do so both for its own citizens and for the international community in general. In order to be recognized as a responsible international actor it has first to be accepted at home. Its constituents must accept that the Union is effectively acting on their behalf and in their interest. Global change will then have to lead to a globally defined policy: a challenge if there ever was one for the Community turned Union. How does the Union want to go about it? The Treaty of Rome stipulated in its Preamble that the member countries are "resolved to strengthen the safeguards of peace and liberty by establishing this combination of resources and calling upon the other people of Europe who share their ideal to join in their efforts". In the Maastricht Treaty (the famous-infamous Title V) the Community turned Union is more ambitious. Together with its member states it aims at defining and implementing a common foreign and security policy. Among its objectives shall be, so the text goes, "to preserve peace and strengthen international security, in accordance with the principles of the United Nations' Charter as well as the prin-

---

34 Cf. an overview of some of those, partly old but revived, partly new developments (money laundering, organized crime, drug traffic), in: Internationale Politik 2 (1995).

ciples of the Helsinki Final Act and the objectives of the Paris Charter" and "to develop and consolidate democracy and the rule of law, and respect for human rights and fundamental freedoms".

These are lofty goals indeed. To attain them even partially will demand a high degree of common will, consensus and perseverance. The treaty does not specify – and rightly so – at which countries or regions the pursuance of these objectives is directed. It is an open-ended commitment, applicable worldwide or wherever the Union sees either an opportunity or even a necessity to pursue these goals. We can, however, assume that their first and foremost addressee will be what we called the three peripheries: Central and Eastern Europe including Russia and the former Soviet republics, the Mediterranean area and the Balkans. The Union therefore sees itself as an actor in international relations with a message. Its influence is largely determined by the combined weight of its members and the degree of its acting in unison.

So far, so good. But the question raised by one observer already some years ago, remains still valid. It is the question whether a group of states can really be recognized as an "effective international actor" in a world of transition with new values and interests emerging. In this author's view, the Community's capabilities "have been talked up to the point where a significant capability-expectations gap exists"[35]. Indeed, between the Union's proclaimed intentions and its actual capacity to pursue them effectively, exists a wide gap today. It will, at best, narrow only slowly and as a result of both a gradual convergence of interests and a determined streamlining of the decision making process.

Will the European Union be up to this double challenge? Much of the answer will depend on whether it succeeds in proving that its original idea of unification – symbolized by the Treaty of Rome – is still applicable today.[36] In other words: whether, beyond a certain degree of economic integration within and a step-by-step enlargement outside, it can prove that a united Europe can become an effective international actor capable of pursuing the mission it has set to itself.

---

35 Christopher Hill, The Capability-Expectations Gap, or Conceptualizing Europe's International Role, in: Journal of Common Market Studies (September 1993), p. 306.
36 A pertinent question raised in the article by Wolfgang Wessels, Rationalizing Maastricht: the search for an optimal strategy of the new Europe, in: International Affairs (July 1994), p. 454.

Reviewing enlargement

The next new concerns are closer home. There is, first, the already much debated fifth enlargement. There is no disrespect in saying that by admitting countries like Poland, the Czech Republic and Hungary into the Union, the latter is not only taking an important step, but also opening up a new chapter in its history. For the first time it will receive countries with a communist past. In the forty-five years of Soviet imposed communism these countries developed, surely much against their own grain, bureaucratic habits, political outlooks and social networks which are not easy to throw overboard, let alone forget overnight.

To admit countries like Austria or Sweden was hardly more than continuing the *courant normal*. In spite of their neutral status, these countries had formed an integral part of Western Europe in all but foreign and defence matters. Now to admit a country like Poland or Slovakia will be different in various, though surely not all respects. Their – perfectly understandable – desire to join the Union is one thing. Their capacity of understanding concepts like federalism and integration is another. Forty years of close cooperation, accommodation and consensus building within the Union represent a capital that, for no fault of their own, these countries were unable to accumulate in their own, Soviet-dominated world. To some the notion of nation is different from that in Western countries; in most the idea of regional cooperation has rarely, if ever taken root. These concepts and realities are new to them. They have to be acquired and learned, understood and practiced – no less than in fact previous newcomers to the Community had to do.

By opening its doors to Central and Eastern Europe, the Union will therefore also open a new chapter in its existence. In three respects. First, with regard to its own internal cohesion and external orientation. Second, with regard to its place and role in a continent that henceforth will know two categories of countries: those who are in – and those who are out. Finally, and as a consequence of this, the Union will have to state how it sees its relationship with Russia (and other CIS countries) and the latter's place on the continent.

94

Defining Russia's role

Indeed, the question about the place and role of Russia in Europe is as old as the Russian/Soviet empire itself. Russia, in her Czarist as well as in her Soviet version, was and is part of Europe but always wanted to be something more. She saw herself as bastion of the Christian-Orthodox faith but also as the successor to Rome and Constantinople – the 'Third Rome'. Both the Czars and Stalin offered their country as the *gendarme de l'Europe*, but also considered it as the defender against the 'Golden Hordes' from Asia. Russia saw herself, in other words, as being part of Europe and Asia at the same time. In Mackinder's words, she is the world's "heartland", straddled between the two continents and reaching at times even into the Middle East.[37] For reasons of her size and location, her internal heterogeneity and her imperial ambitions, Russia as a power is impossible to integrate into any community but equally impossible to ignore. She is simply too big and too self-reliant to qualify as a member of the European Union even if both sides wanted it – which neither obviously does.

The Union's concern must therefore be to develop with Russia (and no less with Ukraine) a stable relationship that takes into account this dichotomy. It should offer Russia the role and influence that she needs for her internal stabilization and her external security. In other words, Russia should be offered her 'due' without being given a veto when it comes to deciding on the destinies of her neighbours or indeed the confines of an enlarging European Union.

To strike the right balance between consideration for Russia's special status and interests on the one hand, and respecting the desire of Central and East European countries to join the Union on the other, is not going to be an easy task. It requires on the part of the latter a double track strategy: one of conditional membership for countries east of the former dividing line, and one of conditioned partnership with Russia and Ukraine. Together, these two groups should ideally serve as building blocs for an as yet fragmented and economically divided continent.

---

37 Halford J. Mackinder, The Geographical Pivot of History, in: Geographical Journal, Vol. XXIII (1904), pp. 421–444.

Such double objectives require a balancing act both in a figurative and a real sense. In a situation of great fluidity and uncertainty, its progress and outcome are uncertain.

Nobody can say with any certainty how many members the Union will eventually count and what its internal organization will be. Nor can we say anything definitive about the future nature of transatlantic relations and the direction United States foreign policy will take. And indeed, who would venture to offer more than an educated guess about the future shape and organization of Europe as a whole? In this sense, the really new concern for the Union is its uncertainty about itself and that of Europe.

Preventing conflicts

The fourth concern is again old and new at the same time. It has to do with the prevention or resolution of conflicts on the continent. Periods of stability and peace in Europe were more often than not the exception rather than the rule. Practically all attempts to pacify and unify at least parts of it, either by force or by negotiation, failed. Empires came and went. They did so usually in the wake of devastating wars. The apotheosis of all this came in the twentieth century. Two world wars ended Europe's global dominance but also, thankfully, the era of major international wars. Thus, the last empire, the Soviet Union, ended with a whimper rather than with a blow. Wars at its periphery tell us, however, that with major wars improbable, small conflicts remain on Europe's agenda. Geographically, they may seem remote to most Europeans, politically they are not.

The Union, all too sudden after the hopeful days of fall 1989, saw itself confronted with conflicts for which it had not been prepared. In this situation – and no doubt under the shock of the Yugoslav tragedy – the idea of 'preventive diplomacy' finds a growing number of supporters. To be sure, every government – and no less any international organization concerned with peace and security – prefers conflict prevention to actual conflicts. That is after all what an important part of diplomacy is all about. The Union was, rightly or wrongly, severely criticized for precisely having failed in this task in Yugoslavia. No doubt that either as a Union or through some of its members it could have done more to stem the country's inexorable drift towards disintegration and eventually war. To do so the Union lacked the political consensus and, perhaps even more seriously, the necessary intelligence and analytical set-up indispensable to anticipate events and act in time.

Having said all this, the notion of preventive diplomacy is misleading in many respects. It suggests that diplomatic activity is the sole and sufficient means to forestall what usually is the result of many and diverse developments. Most of them require different treatment with different means. If preventive measures would therefore be the more appropriate term when it comes to preventing conflicts, it would require a wide panoply of tools and policies. This is something that the Union in its present state, either on its own or together with the Commission, simply does not have at its disposal. We will therefore have to be quite modest when judging the Union's capacity for conflict prevention. We may regret it in view of the many potential conflicts that seem still to be in store in tomorrow's Europe. Yet we had better accept this insufficiency as a given so as to spare ourselves undue disappointments.

The disintegration of the Soviet Union and of Yugoslavia, and the divorce between the Czech Republic and Slovakia left the continent more fragmented than it has been for a long time. People freed from the discipline of hegemony and the fear of military intervention, claim the right of self-determination. The individualization of particular interests, mostly in the name of precisely this Wilsonian self-determination and spurred by easy access to arms, facilitates escalation of even minor tensions into open conflicts. They are difficult to control and even more difficult to end. Not all may be as cruel as the civil war in former Yugoslavia. What happened in Chechnya in the winter of 1994/95 will make us, however, cautious in our predictions. At least it shows that the horrors of some peoples' wars do not deter other people from repeating them.

For the first time, the European Union is now challenged to take position in and on conflicts. It has to state how it sees its role in such conflicts and whether it is prepared to prevent or resolve them. It may claim that they are beyond its legal and political reach. But it finds it increasingly difficult, if not impossible, to declare that they are beyond its moral responsibility or concern. Once this is said and done, comes the crucial test for the Union's much invoked CFSP according to Article J.4 of the Maastricht Treaty, and its credibility in times of crisis and conflict.

It would be nice to state that in the Yugoslav crisis the Union has stood this test. It has not. The strains within it were often as severe as the failures without. For a while it seemed that the crisis would split the Union. Old rivalries over influence in the Balkans re-emerged. Almost forgotten 'special relationships', believed to be dead, seemed to surface again. For some time it seemed that Germany's (and Austria's) sympathies for Croatia were awakening again, running against those of France and Britain for Serbia and leaving Italy somewhere on the sideline – an Italy that insists on having still unsettled business with Slovenia. Russia in turn made clear its sympathy for Slavonic and orthodox Serbia while Greece found it difficult to recognize diplomatically a country that insisted on being called Macedonia as does the Northern part of Greece herself. Split loyalties thus enter in conflict with common history; old faultlines of religious and ethnic divisions re-emerge and unforgiven counts of previous massacres are now being settled in the brutal way. All this was bound to affect the immediate neighbourhood and eventually Europe as a whole. The Union was, if not paralysed by these revived ghosts of European history, then surely sorely tested. What many had feared now threatened to become a reality: crisis management not as a helping hand for the conflicting parties in need but as a source of strain and suspicion amongst those supposed to stretch this hand.

Thankfully, dissent and predilections were in the end not strong enough to wreck the fragile boat of the Union's consensus building. But the flag of warning had gone up. The Yugoslav crisis showed the thin ice on which the CFSP has to be built and developed. The crisis is still far from being over. New demands for help, if not intervention from here, or indeed elsewhere, may arrive at the Union's headquarters. And they are likely to come not just from the East or South-East. The European Union is, after all, faced with three peripheries, as discussed above. There is, to be sure, the fragmented East, the conflict-prone Balkans and, not to be forgotten, the turbulent Mediterranean. They all may require action, either separately or all at the same time. They do so because all of them are convinced, rightly or wrongly, that Brussels has, or should have, the potential for help.

Re-invigorating transatlantic relations

Last but not least: transatlantic relations. Reforming and adjusting them has been on the Community's agenda throughout the Cold War. Western Europe's links, mainly through the Atlantic Alliance, to North America were one of the central features in this now bygone world of East-West confrontation. It was a solid relationship but constantly in need some repair, additional consolidation and mutual assurance of solidarity. Still, the so-called West had its common values and interests. It formed, to use Karl Deutsch's well-known term, a security community. As such it had its distinct features and developed its own culture. This set it clearly apart from the Soviet-communist bloc and indeed from the rest of the world.

Much, but not all of this ended with the end of the Cold War. The frontlines in Europe have disappeared. The Alliance solemnly declared that East and West, North and South would henceforth again be nothing more than indicators of geographic direction. The Paris Charter of the CSCE provided the guidelines for all those willing to join this ever widening community of like-minded democracies. Inevitably, the question arose what kind of specific features the Alliance still could claim to provide as glue for its internal cohesion and justify its continuing existence.

Common defence against an unknown enemy will surely not do. Nor the sheer habit of working together in the classic field of military security. At the same time, the European Union has become both larger in membership and more ambitious in its mission. While still weak in defence and foreign policy, it is recognized by the United States as the most important partner and interlocutor in European, if not in world affairs. Not surprisingly, then, that calls for a new and broader transatlantic pact are becoming more frequent.[38] Some European governments have come up with a proposal for creating a 'Euro-American community' cemented by both security and economic ties. The rationale behind this proposal is twofold: first, to give the increased weight of the economy in world affairs its due, and, second, to broaden the basis for a continuing American presence on the continent beyond its military dimension. The latter no doubt for reasons of balance in a Europe of great political fluidity and uncertainty, and for a European Union whose military muscle is still weak if not absent. Together, so the argument goes, the newly invigorated and broadened Alliance may be better equipped to face up to the new tasks in Europe's Eastern half – primarily extending security cooperation to all those countries in Central and Eastern Europe who want or need it. At the same time such an additional tie to Europe may counteract America's temptation for unilateralism – a temptation nurtured by the belief of many Americans that their country has given the world – and Europe – more than its due and can now wait for the world – and Europe – to pay it back.

Working out a new transatlantic relationship is not going to be an easy task. Desirable as it may be, it is bound to put the Union to a demanding test. The reason for this is that the views of its members about the necessity and scope of such a pact differ. It may be possible to reconcile them eventually. What will, however, be much more difficult is to assuage fears that such close association with the United States could drag the Union into global adventures over which it will have little control or simply have to follow the American lead and finally end up with external failure and internal tension. Under these circumstances it may be wiser to proceed from the opposite angle: not closer association but a better division of labour. Or, as an American observer puts it: "In the past, the most important things that the West Europeans and Americans did were the things they did together. Now, it may well happen that the most important things they do are those

38 Cf. Western Europe Proposes New Trans-Atlantic Pact, in: International Herald Tribune, 7 February 1995; Gunther Heumann, Die Europäische Union und Nordamerika nach Maastricht und GATT – Braucht die Atlantische Gemeinschaft einen neuen Transatlantischen Vertrag ?, in: Interne Studien, No. 70, Konrad-Adenauer-Stiftung, Dezember 1994.

they do apart". His argument is that the alliance must "defeat a force more powerful than the Soviet Union: the force of history"[39] – or, put differently, it must not take the successful common experience of the Cold War as a guide for its relationship in the future. The international environment has changed for the allies as well. What worked in times of confrontation may not necessarily work in times of generalized co-operation. Division of labour does not mean separation. It can or should mean a more rational calculation of the costs and benefits for each side when it comes to deciding who can do better in a specific field than the other – and vice-versa. In the end a mixture of both closer transatlantic cooperation in some fields and a sensible division of labour in others may be the outcome. Even so, this represents no less of a challenge to the Union when it comes to finding a workable balance between the two.

Here again, the yawning gap becomes visible between what the Union should and what it actually can do. Faced with such new tasks or projects, it has to weigh their actual costs for its internal cohesion against the potential benefits for its external position. This is a calculation that, more often than not, could get the Union into the embarrassing situation of having to opt against the latter.

Foreign policy: divisive or unifying?

Foreign policy or, better perhaps, political involvement abroad, can have two contradictory effects: either a unifying or a dividing one. A challenge or threat that concerns all member states more or less alike, can close their ranks and stimulate common action. A situation which in turn is seen or affects interests in different ways, can have the opposite effect. It stirs up animosities and awakens conflicting memories. In the end it blocs consensus.

The more the Union will be exposed to, or drawn into, external events, the more it will be exposed to conflicting pressures, both from

---

39 Cf. W. R. Smyser, The Europe of Berlin, Bertelsmann Foundation Publishers, Gütersloh 1995, pp. 13 ss. Quoted in International Herald Tribune, 18 February 1993.

within and from without. Its obligation, legal or moral, to act will grow. And so will the risk of internal dissent and external disappointment. Conversely, the chances of success will be the greater where interests and perceptions converge or are even identical; the risks of failure will be high where there is little or no convergence that thus makes consensus improbable.

Perhaps, then, the real centre of concern is to be found within the Union itself. It has less to do with the advent of untoward external crises or the new areas of concern and challenges – unpleasant or demanding as they may be – that the Union will be faced with. Rather, it is the Union's own diversity and heterogeneity, the multitude of cultural traditions, political sensitivities and economic priorities that render it so vulnerable to squabbling and eventually weak action. Where they converge and clash, they can become a major, if not insurmountable obstacle to forming and, more difficult still, sustaining a common policy over a long or even indefinite period of time. Unless perceived as a common threat or challenge and thus requiring a common response, crises like the one in former Yugoslavia or those we may have to expect in the Mediterranean, may be more divisive than unifying in their effect. They disintegrate more than they integrate. Or, as the Union's Commissioner for External Relations, Hans van den Broek, formulated it: "The Yugoslav drama has traumatised West European peoples and done more damage to the process of European unity than the hassle about Maastricht. Until now, Europe's divisions have only helped convince the Serbs that they have nothing to worry about.[40]

A severe judgement indeed. It reflects deep frustration about the Union's impotence when faced with a conflict of the Yugoslav kind. Time and later events may attenuate its sharpness. But it lays open the as yet unmitigated weakness of the Union's foreign policymaking process. It demonstrates that there is still an unbridgeable gap between the Union's legal authority and its moral responsibility, between its inherent diversity of outlooks and the desirable if not indispensable need for action.

40 Quoted in International Herald Tribune, 18 February 1993.

It would be neither helpful nor fair to blame these contradictions on an incomplete and quite cumbersome institutional set-up for the conduct of what is still years apart from a truly common foreign and security policy. As long as member countries themselves find it difficult to delegate more of their sacred authority in these two fields to the Union, every exhortation that the latter ought to assume more responsibilities is bound to end up in disappointment. As there is no serious alternative to the Union in sight, and national *démarches* will no longer do, set-backs and frustrations are perhaps the only forces that will push the Union towards what, in the end, looks like a common foreign policy. There are, to be sure, enough new centres of concern that, in addition to the old ones, may make such policy eventually inevitable.

This chapter should, however, not end on too pessimistic a note. To be sure, from many points of view – and in the light of recent experiences (from the Gulf via the Middle East to former Yugoslavia) – the record of the Union's foreign and security policy is far from brilliant. But it is not hopeless either. Its disappointing performance in Yugoslavia has not split the Union. Nor indeed has it discouraged the fifteen member states to pursue their search for common action. The bitter experience in the Balkans may have left scars and re-awakened suspicions with probably all parties concerned. At the same time such tests, once weathered, are useful in laying open loopholes and deficiencies in the process of consultation and decision-making. They reveal where there is sand in the machinery, hidden so far, but also where there are potentially strong points to build upon and develop further. In the complex and complicated institutional Brussels set-up there are surely many things which should – and can – be streamlined. The Community has, often enough, progressed by way of crises or, better perhaps, their management. There is no reason to believe that this will be different in the future. Foreign and security policy is an ideal testing ground for such management. From here progress can hopefully follow in the direction of a more united and constructive European stand on issues that are of central concern to both the continent itself and the world at large.

VI. Forms and Limits of Foreign Policy-Making

"The European Community is the only organized expression of European will and ability in foreign policy."[41] This statement comes from somebody who has been in charge of pushing along a token of common foreign policy, Ambassador Jannuzzi. He was the head of what used to be, until the entry into force of the Maastricht Treaty, the European Political Cooperation Secretariat. His statement implies at least two things: first, that nowhere in Europe outside the Community does one find a platform or an institution capable of identifying, formulating and executing something that reflects an interest shared by European states; second, that there is such a European will and that it should be given the institutional set-up to express itself.

Probably everybody can go along with the first point. Doubts are justified about the second. Europe is simply too heterogeneous ever to develop anything like a common will. The real issue here is, as discussed before, whether we can expect such a common will to develop at least within the European Union and, if so, on which issues it will crystallize and through which policies and institutions it will find its expression. The limitations to such a common will become quickly visible when we look at the way common positions on foreign and security issues are being worked out amongst the member states. More often than not they result in declarations of many words and few deeds.

41 Giovanni Jannuzzi, Scope and Structure of the Community's Future Foreign Policy, in: Reinhardt Rummel (ed.), Toward Political Union, Baden-Baden 1992, p. 289.

This is not the place to review once more both the history of the Community's foreign policy-making process or indeed the meandering debates about its institutionalization, successes and failures. There is already abundant literature on these issues.[42] Practically all authors agree on the desirability, if not necessity of at least some common *foreign*, if not also common *defence* policy. At the same time they conclude that, in spite of progress in the right direction, such a policy is still more a wish than a reality.

Indeed, member states themselves are not quite sure whether they would like the Union, let alone the Commission, to be and act as an independent player in areas where they would still much prefer to act on their own. As long as this is so, clouds of doubt and ambivalence will hang over the Union as an international actor in its own right and with the necessary backing of its members. "Western Europe (here: the European Union) is neither a fully-fledged state-like actor nor a purely dependent phenomenon in the contemporary international arena"[43] – a statement as valid today as when it was made five years ago, i.e. before the conclusion of the Treaty on the European Union. No doubt, the Union is present in some fields. It acts in unison or on behalf of its members in other fields. And it can move on its own in those fields for which it has both the competence and the open or tacit approval of its members. But all this adds still up to what the American political scientist Stanley Hoffmann called a rather "messy phenomenon".

The reluctance of the member states to delegate important sectors of their foreign policy-making power to the Union and its Commission is thus all too noticeable. It finds its reflection in the procedures and institutions needed for making the CFSP actually work.[44] At first

---

42 Cf. Reinhard Rummel (ed.), Toward Political Union, Baden-Baden 1992; Hugh Miall, Shaping a New European Order, Chatham House Papers, London, 1994; Josef Janning, Außen- und Sicherheitspolitik nach Maastricht, in: Werner Weidenfeld (ed.), Maastricht in der Analyse, Gütersloh 1994, pp. 55–69; Elfriede Regelsberger (ed.), Die Gemeinsame Außen- und Sicherheitspolitik der Europäischen Union, Bonn 1993. More specifically on security policy Matthias Jopp. The Strategic Implications of European Integration, Adelphi Paper 290, International Institute for Strategic Studies, London, July 1994.
43 David Allen and Michael Smith, Western Europe's presence in the contemporary international arena, in: Review of International Studies 16 (1990), p. 20.
44 Cf. Table IX in the annex.

glance, one must assume, or fear, that the further enlargements are likely to slow down the former and complicate the reform of the latter.

Declaratory policy

The CFSP, like its predecessor, the European Political Cooperation, is supposed to serve several functions and operate according to different objectives.[45] First, the Union can act by declarations and *démarches* explaining its position. This is no doubt an important function in a double sense: it obliges member countries to address jointly a particular issue on which they have jointly to take a stand; furthermore, such a declaration or *démarche* demonstrates *urbi et orbi* that the Union cannot, or will not, remain indifferent in face of important events in its international environment. The Community has enunciated numerous statements of the kind. They range from admonitions to the Soviet Union about its invasion of Afghanistan to its warnings to the conflictual parties in former Yugoslavia.

Nobody expects immediate and tangible results of such declaratory acts. They are manifestations of displeasure or concern. As such they perform the function of an *acte de présence* on part of the Union. Whether it likes it or not, the Union and its members have to take a stand on international issues that are of political or moral importance. Indifference or silence is no attitude a community of democratic states can afford. It is even less so on issues that are likely to move the hearts and minds of their citizens. The intrusion of foreign affairs into domestic politics – and vice versa – is a development which no government can ignore without risking its own survival.

The drama in Yugoslavia, so close to the Union's border was probably a watershed. Coinciding with the end of the Cold War it has made West Europeans feel more responsible for, and responsive to, events in what used to be the communist – and therefore hostile – part of the continent. Now the Union simply cannot remain silent anymore even

---

45 For the following cf. Reinhardt Rummel, EPZ – Erfolgsformel für die Gemeinsame Europäische Außenpolitik? Stiftung Wissenschaft und Politik Ebenhausen, April 1987, pp. 32ss; Simon Nutall. European Political Co-operation, Oxford 1992.

if it does not have the power and the tools to act in more than merely a symbolic way.

Even if gratuitous, such declarations and actions have their utility. As a minimum, they serve as a kind of 'training ground' for the member states in foreign policy-making. They keep in motion the respective ministries, council and officials. They provide the incentive to anticipate events and hammer out common positions. All this, laborious and often perfunctionary, generates routine. It oils the heavy machinery of CFSP and narrows down differences that otherwise may impede action. Still, too many hollow-sounding declarations and symbolic *démarches* without tangible follow-up action tend to become harmful. They not only weaken the impact of the Union's statements. More seriously, they can undermine its credibility as an international actor.

Conference diplomacy

Second, the Union is becoming ever more present as a player in conference diplomacy. It is in the fora of international conferences and the corridors of innumerable institutions that it can bring to bear the weight of a common position of its members. It did so, probably for the first time in such a concerted way, during the first GATT trade negotiations, the so-called Kennedy Round in 1964.

But before the Community is able to come up with a common position, many internal negotiations and much horse-trading amongst its members are needed. There are highly sensible issues and interests at stake: a common trade policy even of a relatively homogeneous group of countries is no child's play. To keep a common position intact throughout prolonged and tedious negotiations and in a forum like WTO puts a lot of strain on all members and the Community in the first place. Intra-Community negotiations thus test both the cohesiveness of the Community itself and no doubt that of its main trading partners, the United States and Japan. Still it has its benefits. It lays open the communality of interests as well as the differences of policies of the member states with the aim of arriving finally at a commonly acceptable denominator. Because once such consensus has been reached, the Union can pull its full weight. The price for such consensus may, however, be a more restricted capacity for concessions. From the Kennedy Round, just mentioned, throughout the prolonged and painful negotiations in the Uruguay Round the Community must have accumulated a wealth of experience in multilateral trade fora. With this may possibly come a certain amount of inside resentments but, equally and more importantly, also a manifestation of credibility outside. Here as in other cases where the Union acts as a single entity, the process of attaining a common goal together may be as important as the goal itself.

In the Conference on Security and Cooperation in Europe it found itself in unchartered territory. It had to address, in addition to economic issues, political and security questions. It was a novel experience. As the CSCE became a quasi-permanent operation, the Community's CSCE diplomacy, too, developed its own routine and profile. Over the years, the Community thus grew into something resembling a 'bloc'. At least so it was perceived by those who were not its members. Despite occasional divergencies of views and clashes of interests, the nine and later twelve members acquired a weight of their own. It was often more important than that of NATO and surely that of the Warsaw Pact. Once the Twelve had succeeded in agreeing on a common position, other states found it difficult to oppose, let alone to reverse it. No group had to accept this more grudgingly, or at least reluctantly, than the neutral and non-aligned countries – the N+N group as it was called. It came to realize that once either the erstwhile superpowers, the United States and the Soviet Union, or the European Community, or even the two together, had made up their minds, it was nearly impossible to modify a thus established position. It then mattered little that the CSCE was supposed to be an assembly of thirty-five states of formally equal status and vote.

Conference diplomacy thus develops its own momentum for the Community's foreign policy writ large. It draws member states into a continuing process of learning, consultation and consensus-building. Rules of the game are developed, personal relationships set up, habits evolved and procedures adopted. Over the years, all this becomes a generally accepted routine. It creates, partly by intent, partly unconsciously, a kind of 'negotiating culture'. It may not count as one of the most conspicuous achievements of the Community. But it is certainly a useful and endurable one.

By acting in unison in this peculiar world of international organizations, the Community thus gained a weight and an importance of its own. It was, and still is, coveted as a partner for ad-hoc coalitions with third countries. This works also the other way round: the Community is sometimes in need of partners and will be more so as the number of competitors grows, as traditional alliances get under strain or have outlived their usefulness. Coalition building may indeed become more important in a world in which ideological affinities count less than economic complementarity; where political loyalties must cede to financial interests. In such situations the necessity for internal cohesion grows accordingly. The glue of a commonly defined interest must hold lest the Community loses both influence and credibility at the same time.

Clearly, cohesion is more easily attainable and sustainable where consensus can be achieved by way of internal bargaining, by compromise and reciprocal compensation. It is also easier to preserve where all member states have more or less equal status and stakes. This seems to be more the case in international conferences in which economic stakes and political prestige weigh less: many of the United Nations specialized agencies, today possibly also the OSCE, belong to that category. In economic and trade-oriented organizations such as the newly created World Trade Organization or the Bretton Woods institutions, the Union must work harder for a common position. Its essence must be defended under pressure but remain flexible for concessions on the margin.

Another case is the United Nations itself, or, more precisely, the different status enjoyed by France and Britain as permanent members of the Security Council compared with that of the other Union members. As mentioned above such a different status, manifest in an institutionalized difference in power and influence, can, or in fact does, create problems within the Union. It does even more so as, besides the possession of nuclear weapons, neither Britain nor France can pretend to superiority over their partner Germany, and possibly Italy, in any other

110

field, be it economic strength, financial power or population size. It is true that both Britain and France have maintained a tradition of military deployment overseas. It was persuasively demonstrated by their active involvement in the Gulf war of 1990. In former Yugoslavia France and Britain maintain the biggest contingents of peace-keeping forces. Still, this difference of status creates two classes of states within the Union. It cannot be justified except for reasons of pure inertia and incapacity for reform on the part of the United Nations. In times of crises in particular, such a two-class status could become a source of irritation if not also tension within the Union.

Finally, the position of the Union within the Atlantic Alliance. It would seem straightforward at first glance, given the close relationship that developed between Western Europe and North America during the many years of the Cold War. But it is not. And it may become even less straightforward in the years to come.

Europe, as somebody rightly remarked, shares with Russia a continent and with the United States an alliance. The first, for sheer geopolitical reasons, has every chance to remain. The permanence of the second is not assured. That has several reasons. Not all members of the European Union are also members of the Alliance. That has been the case of Ireland and is now the case of the newcomers Austria, Finland and Sweden. Furthermore, as mentioned before, views on the future of the Alliance diverge. There are those who recognize its declining strategic utility as a consequence of the disappearance of the Soviet-communist threat. On the other hand, there are those who advocate, possibly because of that, an enlargement of the Alliance beyond its erstwhile political-military dimension. And finally, there are people on both sides of the Atlantic who expect Europe to develop in fulfillment of Title V of the Maastricht Treaty, its own security and defence policy. In their view, the European Union should become an adult, capable of taking care of its own security needs rather than relying forever on America's strategic protection. Europe's security independence would, at long last, add the missing component to its personality as an international actor in its own right. Such elevation in status would not spell the end of the particularly close relationship with the United States. On the contrary, it might even strengthen it by allowing for a more balanced division of labour. Thus, Europe has no ambition to "replicate the US capabilities for large-scale power projection, even if it must remedy some serious deficiencies in its strategic capabilities (in airlift, intelligence and communication").[46]

The hard core of the problem lies elsewhere: in the nuclear field. On its arduous way to becoming a credible international actor the Union will be faced with the question whether or not it will ever become the depository of the French and British nuclear arsenals. They might first be merged and later be put under the command of a politically united Union. President Chirac of France, in early September 1995, revived an idea that, not unlike the monster in Loch Ness, surfaces from time to time merely to disappear because nobody actually believes in it. Chirac offered to expand his country's nuclear umbrella to other European countries, in particular Germany. Logic would indeed argue in favour of not only merging the French-British nuclear forces but of putting them at the disposal of the European Union or rather its members. But the chances for this happening are, for the foreseeable future, slim indeed. There is no European political nor in fact concomitant military authority that would be capable of taking over the command and control of these weapons. One may split the atom but so far nobody is willing to split the control over it. Nor can we take it for granted that all member states are eager to become co-owners of such a nuclear capacity, least of all Germany.

The problem of a 'nuclearized European Union' is raised here because it illustrates, in an unmistakable way, the obstacles to consensus building first and foremost within the Union itself, and then within the Atlantic Alliance. It is in this complex field of command and control of the 'ultimate weapon' in particular, but also of national security in general, that supreme interests of every state come into play. Few, if any of them will ever be put on the table of negotiation. The best we can expect here are moderate degrees of accommodation and multilateral concertation. Both leave a wide margin for dissent, misunderstanding and friction. What seemed paradoxical at first glance –

46 Cf. Bertelsmann Foundation, Research Group on European Affairs and European Commission DG IA, Interim Report of a Working Group on CSFP and the Future of the European Union, July 1995.

namely that within a well-functioning and time-honoured Alliance, it is more difficult to build a coherent community position – turns out to be both natural and almost inevitable: security and defence issues do not lend themselves easily to deep and lasting compromises. At least they do not do so unless imposed by a common political authority whose verdict has to be accepted by all members. We are therefore no longer talking here about conference diplomacy as an instrument of union-building. We are talking here about the way nations see themselves and want to be seen. These are intangible values. Few countries will be ready to lay them on the negotiating table for the sake of reaching a consensus.

Crisis management

The third and the fourth field in which the European Union is engaged today and no doubt will be even more so tomorrow are interlinked. It is first crisis management and then conflict prevention and resolution. In both, the Union's capacity to act in unison and, in doing so, with consequence, will be tested perhaps more than in any other field.

In his well-remembered speech on the 'Year of Europe' in early 1973, the then Secretary of State, Henry Kissinger, defined Europe as basically a regional actor. In a sense, he was right. Compared to the strategic power and reach of his own country, the United States, and the Soviet Union, Europe could claim neither. To be sure, both France and Britain retained residues of former colonial grandeur and a modicum of military forces and presence that went with it. Also Europe retained, or claimed to do so, global interests. They are, however, more economic than strategic. As a consequence, Europe was, and still is, vulnerable to events outside its reach but likely to hurt its interests: the October War of 1973 with its ensuing oil embargo dramatically illustrated this vulnerability. A few exceptions apart (French Black Africa being one of them) European states cannot claim to have the capability and reach to prevent crises in distant areas or manage them if they occurred. Britain's intervention in the distant Falkland islands may have been the last – or surely one of the last – single-handled military

113

actions beyond Europe's geographic confines. While executed with great bravura, it turned out to be a very costly expedition. The chances of it being repeated are slim.

All this is to say that for Europe, or the European Union, the days of imperial engagement worldwide are over. No surprise then, that in the last twenty years or so, the Community's reaction to the manifold international crises in the world was rarely one of active engagement in any strategic-military sense. In most cases it was late in time and diplomatic in form. To be sure, the Community could not – and in fact did not – remain silent in face of major international crises. As mentioned before, the OPEC oil embargo of 1973 was amongst the first to induce the Community, at its Copenhagen summit, to formulate a common position on a central political issue, namely its relations with the Arab world and its policy with regard to the Arab-Israeli conflict.

The evolution toward a European Political Cooperation turned out to be a long and often disappointingly slow progress. From here it was again a long way to the new destination, the CFSP. But even with this refurbished and more crafty instrument the Union is still far from being anything like a 'crisis manager'. It has neither the capacity to anticipate international crises, nor does it have a pre-ordained mandate to deal with them if and when they erupt.

Preventive diplomacy

Closely related to, but not identical with crisis management is what now is called preventive diplomacy or, more correctly, preventive measures. Diplomacy alone is not enough when it comes to locating emerging crises and deploying the full panoply of measures that might hopefully prevent them. It is in any case a delicate task. It requires a high degree of political skill and diplomatic sensitivity not only to detect and identify potentially critical developments but also to not unduly alarm the country or region in question; to avoid the trap of appearing interventionist or indifferent, and to have at one's disposal the necessary means and qualified personnel to steer the parties concerned towards negotiations and settlement.

114

To do all this effectively requires a high degree of purposefulness both as regards the action and the objective the action should attain. The Union, with the combined support of its members, could play an important role in such missions of preventive action. Since the end of the Cold War, expectations rose that the Union would in fact do precisely that. So far the number of missions it took on itself, remains more than modest.[47] Perhaps its assistance in South Africa's first general elections in 1994 can be quoted here. The Union's role in the Yugoslav crisis on the other hand was less fortunate. The reasons for this are surely complex. But they point to one problem as yet unsolved: the often conflicting interests of member countries when it comes to dealing with specific countries or issues. Old memories revive and old rivalries interfere in what ought to be a joint action and determined action. History stands in its way. Having said this, there is no reason why the Union, by trial and error, should not gradually develop a consensus on how preventive actions can be carried out more forcefully with the joint support of all members rather than with an *Alleingang* i.e. with each of them proceeding on its own.[48]

Growing pressure for common action

As long as the Union is still far from being anything like a state, it has no other choice than to improve on what it has and what it is possible of attaining in the foreseeable future. It has made great strides in fields in which it could play out its strength both as a community of Twelve and as an economic power. It has gained notable weight in international fora and negotiations, in direct negotiations with individual countries and in multilateral contexts like the Lomé Convention. Its principal and possibly enduring weakness, however, comes to the open if and when it has to act as a political unit: in crisis management, conflict prevention and conflict resolution. Sadly enough, it is precisely

47 Cf. Table X in the annex.
48 Cf. for a detailed analysis of the Union's crisis management: Trevor C. Salmon, Testing times for European Political Cooperation. The Gulf and Yugoslavia. 1990–1992 in: International Affairs (1992), pp. 233–253.

in these latter fields where the Union's contribution will be in particular demand: first, when it comes to confronting the task of stabilizing the wider Europe, then, when the peripheries are in need of help, and, finally, when the world at large will call for its due. On all three accounts the transition from sheer impotence to real power promises to be long but inevitable. To embark on it with some expectations of success will therefore demand a great deal of imagination but surely also a greater amount of integration.

The potential for more concrete and pointed action is no doubt available. Thus, earlier in the Yugoslav crisis, a concerted warning of the Union to both Croatia and Serbia, accompanied with the threat of economic sanctions, might have made a difference. More recently, the Union has made clear, although all too timidly, its misgivings about President Yeltsin's brutal use of force against Chechnya. The possibility that its aid to Russia would have to be reviewed was at least alluded to. More concretely, the European Parliament, in a rare show of consensus and concern, postponed the ratification of the Union's partnership agreement with Russia until the Chechnya crisis would be settled in a satisfactory way. These and similar actions or rather reactions, may not fundamentally change the course of events. But they signal both the presence and attentiveness of the Union in times and locations of tensions in which it is expected to take an interest. They also demonstrate its capability to act not just as a mere addition of fifteen national wills but as an expression of common interests.

In a different field, the Union could strengthen joint export controls of its members for major weapons systems and, why not, the particularly insidious anti-personnel mines. In fact, on April 10th, 1995, the Union's foreign ministers recommended in unison the indefinite extension of the Non-Proliferation Treaty. A month later, at the NPT-conference in New York, they acted accordingly casting their voice in favour of such extension. But shortly afterwards they showed less cohesion when French President Chirac announced the resumption of nuclear tests in the South Pacific. Timid protests by some and embarrassed silence by others showed how fragile unanimity can become when an important member country acts on its own, without prior consultation and in a matter that it considers to be of its own utmost national interest. Nowhere is such temptation of going alone greater than in the military-defence field in general, in nuclear issues in particular. It is here where pride and prejudice, prestige and status weigh most heavily.

But movement towards more concertation does not seem impossible. The international environment has, since the end of the Cold War become less antagonistic. At the same time it has made states more alert to the risks of weapons proliferation and the dangers of internal conflicts. If the Union is not yet in a position to apply jointly political pressure – whose impact is all the greater if combined with the credible threat of use of force – then the Union must at least attempt to strengthen all other mechanisms by which such a diffusion of military power – be it weapons of massive destruction or light weapons – can be prevented, and violations of human rights sanctioned.

If 'positive' political power – behind which more often than not stands the threat of use of force – cannot be employed, the Union could at least try harder and in a more systematic way to prevent crises from erupting, arms being used indiscriminately, and violations of human rights being committed without penalty. If military force hurts immediately, economic sanctions hurt over a longer period of time, and perhaps more lastingly. Given the enormous economic and financial weight the Union can muster on the one hand, and the glaring economic vulnerabilities of most of its neighbours and many more distant partners on the other, there is no reason why the Union should not use the first in order to try constructively to influence the behaviour of the latter.

VII. A Role in the World: Between Ideal and Reality

The European Community has never been short of good intentions. It has pledged, time and again, to be what the outside world expected it to be, namely a potentially strong player on the international scene, commensurate with the economic weight it represents. It has made some headway in becoming a political force of its own: first, by the mere fact of its very existence and continuing development; second, by its economic power that casts a political shadow and generates political responsibilities the Union cannot refuse and the outside world expects.

Progress in foreign policy making has come in leaps and bounds. On balance, it was modest, not always coherent and, above all, short of having a lasting impact. Formulating a common stand on policy issues required either a dramatic crisis or prolonged negotiations. The former remained the exception, the latter became the rule. The Treaty on the European Union opened the door to new possibilities of action. The Union's external relations could, at least in theory, move now into 'cruising speed'. It has, in the words of a high official of the Commission, embarked on the "slow path to global power".[49]

---

49 Günther Burghardt, The European Union – A Global Power in the Making? (Manuscript Brussels 1994).

119

More members – more responsibilities

It is an open question whether and how the Community's successive enlargements affected its external standing and policy. Surely, the accessions of, first, Britain, Denmark and Ireland (in 1973), then of Greece (in 1981), of Spain and Portugal (in 1986) and, most recently (1995) of Austria, Finland and Sweden change the nature of the animal. They introduced into the Community new and often conflicting traditions, interests and outlooks. At the same time, the sheer expansion in space is adding political weight to what the Union says and does. Almost imperceptively, it is driven to assume a role internationally which at least some of its members are either not capable or not willing to assume individually. In a sense, the Union is acquiring a new quality: twelve, and now fifteen member states – and possibly twenty tomorrow – act and react differently then do only six.

External enlargement does therefore not just call for internal adjustment or reform. It increases at the same time the importance of the Union as an international actor. In so doing, it raises expectations as to what such a constantly growing actor ought to do. Put very simply: the Union does not live in a vacuum in which it can grow and prosper without this having an impact on its environment. Of course, it has. The environment, i.e. the international community reacts, either positively or negatively, with concern or hope. It will judge the Union by comparing its potential to its performance, and measure its declarations by their effects.

Is it totally unfair to state that, so far, the gap seems wide between the challenges the Union is faced with, and its capacity to deal with them; between the expectations directed at the Union, and its response so far; between the urgency for its acting efficiently, and the slowness of its decision-making? The jury is still out. But it would seem that it will become more severe in its judgement as time passes on.

The answer to all this is that what the Union should, or could, ideally do, is still far from daily reality. In a way, the Union suffers from 'overstretch'. It is surely not 'imperial overstretch' – a term used to describe the various reasons for the decline of the two Cold War superpowers, the United States and the former Soviet Union. To use it in

120

connection with the European Union does, of course, in no way imply that the Union is anywhere near an 'imperial policy' nor hopefully will ever be. If there is overstretch then it is either one *avant la lettre* or one 'in reverse'. *Avant la lettre* because the Union finds itself committed or expected to accomplish objectives for which it is either not yet prepared or does not have the means required. It is presumed to act as a great power before even being close to looking anything like a state. Inevitably, growing tensions result between what the Union is expected or at least hoped to do and what it actually can do. Whatever its precise *finalité politique* or eventual prime objective may be – and we will have to come back to that – it would seem that it is still far from being backed up by the political unity and the institutional set-up that are indispensable for pursuing it. Hence the overstretch between 'power to be' and 'power in being'.

The other kind of overstretch implies that the Union may have the means to do many things but has not, or not yet, actually the will to use these means to the maximum of their potential. We call it 'overstretch in reverse' because we have here just the opposite of what great powers used to do: while still keeping alive the will for global reach they were losing the potential to translate it into action. Theirs was not a lack of political will but an eroding material base to project and impose it. In the European Union just the opposite is the case: its potential for action is often greater than its capacity to act.

Such an historic reminder proves the necessity of marrying material power to political will, of adjusting the institutions to the objectives which they are supposed to serve and attain. For the time being, the Union is still torn between what it is expected to do – and what, given its material resources, it in fact could do – and what it is entitled to do and capable of doing. The desired and desirable transition from economics to politics is either incomplete or has in some instances not yet even taken place. Even if the Union has developed into a political force of its own, as mentioned before, there is still a clear discrepancy between its economic potential and its political performance. Or, in the harsh words of a recent report of a high-level group of experts: "The problem is that there is frankly nothing to show for all this activity, all the fresh starts and 'progress' (sc. of the Union); on the contrary, there is an increasing sense of unease at the impotence and drift highlighted week after week by current issues and their reflection in the media".[50]

In other words: the Union has not yet adjusted to a radically different international environment. It is an environment that, as described above, requires on the part of the Union an overhaul of the way it anticipates events, defines its priorities, formulates its foreign policy, and honours its external commitments. This implies a two-way street: that the Union is as much an object of international politics as an important actor in it. It therefore can neither stay aloof nor remain passive. It has to react as much as it has to act to shape and influence the international environment by recognizing its new shifts and challenges as well as to manifest actively its own interest and preferences.

A new *finalité politique*

It is precisely this interaction between external challenges and internal change, between the need to react and the wish to act, that will oblige the Union, more than ever before, to define its *finalité politique* – the kind of Europe and the kind of world it wants to live in and help to develop, and the ways and means with which it wants to do so.

The first and principal target is and will remain the wider Europe. The desire to pacify, reconstruct and stabilize the continent has provided the *raison d'être* and *finalité*, the basis and mission of the European Community and no less of the Union today. Between the end of the Second World War and the end of the Cold War the Community served four basic goals: the avoidance of any future war amongst European states by way of integration and, above all, Franco-German reconciliation; economic reconstruction of a continent devastated by war, followed by economic development and social welfare in and among the member states; and, finally, as the confrontation with the Soviet bloc sharpened, Western Europe's integration was used both as a shield against, and a convincing platform

---

50 Cf. High level group of experts on the CFSP, European Security policy towards 2000: ways and means to establish genuine credibility, First report, Brussels, 19 February 1994, p. 3.

of competition with, Communism. These four objectives provided the Community with a rationale and *finalité* that amply sufficed to legitimize it *vis-à-vis* its own citizens and *vis-à-vis* the outside world. Together they were strong enough to prevent any doubts about their validity. Much has changed since. War amongst European states has become almost unthinkable.

Western Europe, in spite of occasional periods of recession, is more prosperous than ever. The confrontation and competition with the communist model is over, and Europe's division with it. In other words: the time-honoured objectives, or *finalités*, of the Community turned Union were, in their very essence, attained. And they did so beyond all expectations and dreams so vivid and urgent only forty or even twenty years ago. The reverse of the medal is that in this changed environment the Union has to find a new or at least an additional rationale to justify its mission in the new Europe and to push the internal reforms that should or must follow from it. Citizens must again be convinced that the Union is not just an addition of national interests but is the common denominator and best promoter of European – and that, in the end means: their own personal – interests. Nothing would be more damaging to the cohesion and the mission of the Union than if it were seen, either exclusively or primarily, as either merely amplifying national interests on a European level or legitimizing the renationalization of what should be European interests.

The Union's power and potential lie in the innovative way in which it has achieved not only a single common market but, equally important, moulded the formerly independent states of different size and habits into a community. Nobody can deny that this is a tremendous achievement, occasional fits of tensions and bureaucratic excesses notwithstanding. From here the Union must draw the strength for its future mission. This explains its attraction to the many countries in the waiting room for admission.

But beyond mere enlargement, or at least as a consequence of it, the Union is bound to underpin it by a concept for a new political order in Europe as a whole (what, in German, would be called *eine ordnungspolitische Vorstellung für Gesamteuropa*). Here and nowhere else do we see the new and central *finalité politique* for the Union. It is not only the logical continuation of a process that leads the Community from its original task as pacifier and integrator in Western Europe to become now a cornerstone of a wider and undivided Europe. It is at the same time commensurate with the Union's economic power and the political responsibility that flows from it. This is a tall order. As such it calls for some innovation as well as some qualifications as to its scope and realization.

Common foreign policy without tears?

Few people would contest that, given the fluidity of the present European landscape, the European Union is more in demand than ever. Much, too much perhaps, is expected from this Union. It is supposed to be the nucleus of a future European order of whatever size and scope; a conflict manager and pacifier in areas of potential and actual conflict; a provider of assistance of all kinds to countries in need both on the continent and outside, and, last but not least, a partner and interlocutor when it comes to discussing and handling major international tasks be they in commerce, technology, environment, finance or just simple politics.

So far the expectations and occasionally also their fulfillment. But the CFSP of the Union is far from being able to live up to both the demands of the profoundly changed environment and the expectations that it raises. In many respects it is still a 'paper tiger'.[51] Or, somewhat less scathingly, it can be considered as "a technologically modernized version of old-fashioned alliance diplomacy".[52] In other words: we have to do here with an animal whose nature and identity are as yet difficult to define. The principal reason for this is simply the fact that there is no general and clear agreement on what the body that is in charge of it – namely the European Union – actually is.

---

51 Elfriede Regelsberger, Gemeinsame Außen- und Sicherheitspolitik, in: Jahrbuch der Europäischen Integration 1992/93, Bonn 1993, p. 223.
52 Wolfgang Wessels, Von der EPZ zur GASP – Theoriepluralismus mit begrenzter Aussagekraft, in: E. Regelsberger (ed.), Die Gemeinsame Außen- und Sicherheitspolitik der Europäischen Union, op. cit., p. 16.

Some progress was made on both accounts with the Maastricht Treaty. Its Title V clearly declares the CFSP to be an important pillar of the Union. This led to institutional changes – such as a merging of working groups, the creation of a new directorate general for external affairs within the Commission – as well as to a clearer definition of the Union's 'essential common interests' in external affairs. Thus, the Union's foreign ministers spelled out (in a report submitted to the European Council in Lisbon, in June 1992) three basic criteria by which the Union can determine its common interests: geographic proximity of a certain region or country; an important interest in the political and economic stability of a region or country; and threats to the security of the Union.[53]

Such conceptual clarification and institutional consolidation are both needed and welcome. And yet, as a recent report presented by the Commission concedes "the experience of the CSFP has been disappointing so far ...". While cautioning about too hasty conclusions after only 18 months of its existence, the report adds that "the possibilities have not been used to best effect, owing to the weaknesses of the Treaty, as well as over-restrictive interpretation of its provisions".[54]

These reservations are partly, although more circumspectly, taken up in the Commission's Report for the Reflection Group in view of the forthcoming Intergovernmental Conference 1996. It stresses that the coverage of what is understood to be foreign and security policy was widened by the Treaty. The obligation of member states to align their policies is made more explicit. More common positions were adopted on more issues, and joint actions were more formalized. That means that member states "no longer simply coordinate and align their positions but also aim to act in concert, and in concrete ways". Still the decision-making process remains more often than not 'tortuous and bureaucractic'. There is still confusion about the role of the different instruments the Council wants or is entitled to employ for carrying out

---

53 Cf. Bulletin des Presse- und Informationsamtes der Bundesregierung, No. 71, 1 Bonn, July 1992.
54 Report on the Operation of the Treaty on European Union prepared by the European Commission, Brussels, 10 May 1995.

its joint actions. The net result of all this is, as the report concludes, "the impression that the CFSP lacks coherent form".[55]

To all this have to be added the two crucial points of decision-making and of the functional duplication between the Union and the Community when it comes to traditional negotiations of the latter and the foreign policy making to any effective CSFP. As Britain's former Foreign Secretary Douglas Hurd put it: "Our objective is to exert influence in the world. It is not by way of majority vote that we will get it".[56]

These then, are or probably will be for some time, the limitations and obstacles to the Union's being an international actor in its own right. What the Union tries to do is what might be called a 'foreign policy without tears', i.e. a policy that pretends to serve the interests of all but does not want to harm anybody. In so doing it remains either marginal or symbolic.

No doubt, then: the present situation is both unsatisfactory and ambiguous. The European Union is, as demonstrated here and elsewhere, an international actor and yet it is not in the full sense of the word. It can impose trade sanctions and insist on conditions when it comes to giving assistance and opening up for admission. But surely that is not enough for qualifying as a true policy maker. Today perhaps even less so as the international environment has changed almost beyond recognition. And so have the ways and means to act in the pursuance of one's interests. "Access rather than acquisition, presence rather than rule, penetration rather than possession have become the important issues".[57]

If such is the case – and we think that, on the whole, it is – the mission and nature of foreign policy and the way it is pursued, have changed accordingly. The European Union should take its cue from this. Because in practice this means that 'gun diplomacy' as practiced in various ways by the great powers in the past, has lost much, if not all of its relevance. Conditionality of the economically stronger more

---

55 Intergovernmental Conference 1996, Commission Report for the Reflection Group, Brussels and Luxembourg 1995, p. 61 ss.
56 Süddeutsche Zeitung, 17 June 1995.
57 Wolfgang Hanrieder, Dissolving International Politics – Reflections on the Nation-State, in: American Political Science Review 72 (1978), p 1280, quoted after D. Allen and M. Smith, Western Europe's presence in the contemporary international arena, op. cit., p. 21.

than 'diktat' by the militarily powerful, economic competition more than political confrontation, association more than absorption are gaining weight in international relations. They are precisely the kind of instruments that the Union has at its disposal and can put to use.

How long a 'civil power'?

Here, it would seem, lies the very strength of the Union – at least so far. The Community was – and still mostly is – considered to be what used to be called a 'civil power'[58]: a power that is recognized and respected not because of its military muscle but because of its economic strength. During the Cold War it owed its credibility and acceptability in the Third World precisely to the fact that it was not suspected of pursuing imperial designs and offering protection in exchange for political loyalty.

To some extent this is still true. The European Union, when negotiating treaties of association, gives priority to issues like economic reform, social betterment and political consolidation that matter more than traditional concerns like power and influence. In that sense it is both a 'civil' and a 'civilizing power'.[59] It tries to set standards of behaviour that correspond to its own cultural and political heritage and stem from its beneficial experience with market economy. This is new in international relations inasmuch as such standards are not imposed by force or occupation but transmitted by negotiations and rewarded by pledges of assistance and collaboration. At the same time such a strategy allows the Union to act more like a wealthy multinational company than a politically united entity. But how long can it afford to conduct its foreign policy in such a way in a world in which military force and political clout still matter? How is the Union supposed to act once conflicts appear on the horizon or need to be settled in those very regions in which the Union has, because of their geographic proximity, a special interest?

58 Cf. François Duchêne, Europe's Role in World Peace, in: R. Mayne (ed.), Europe Tomorrow, London 1972; Peter Ludlow, Setting European Community Priorities 1991–1992, London 1991.
59 Christopher Hill, European Political Cooperation considered as Foreign Policy, quoted after D. Allen and M. Smith, Western Europe's Presence in the Contemporary International Arena, op. cit., p. 30.

The moment of truth came in 1991 as the disintegration of Yugoslavia and its impending civil war cast their shadow over the continent. At this moment the Union could no longer avoid the question whether or not a capacity for defence and a capacity for conflict resolution and peace-keeping should be an indispensable part of the much invoked 'European identity'. Or, put differently, can a union, which is not a state proper, pursue anything like a foreign and security policy? If not, what should, and can, be such a union's foreign and security policy? Beyond pious declarations the Union and its fifteen members have so far shied away from giving anything close to a clear-cut answer to these and similar questions. And yet, if the tragic experience in Yugoslavia proves anything, it is precisely the need to clarify the role and responsibility of the Union in tomorrow's Europe. It will have to do so both for its own sake and for that of those outsiders who have a right to know what to expect, or not to expect, from the Union.

Five years after the end of the Cold War Europe as a whole finds itself in a period of transition and uncertainty. This is true for both the future shape and size of the European Union as it is true for the internal development of Russia and its future role and status on the continent. Europe's strategic landscape is still in what an observer called a process of 'autonomisation'[60]: its contours and limitations are no longer determined by the two basically external superpowers. It is Europe itself which has to do it. It is again responsible for the shaping and consolidation of its own architecture – a continuing US presence notwithstanding. Critics will say that the Union has so far done little to shape the still fluid strategic landscape. To be sure, it has opened up to the East and is now also looking southwards. It has, as described above, concluded a whole series of treaties of association and partnership. But it has been hardly sufficiently innovative or daring when it came to going beyond employing its traditional instruments of economic restructuring.[61]

It is true that Europe has never known a single, exclusive tradition

---

60 Dominique David, La Communauté entre la paix et la guerre, in: Politique étrangère 1(1993), p. 81.
61 Cf. a critique of the Union's policy towards the "new Eastern Europe", Heinz Kramer, The European Community's Response to the 'New Eastern Europe', in: Journal of Common Market Studies (June 1993), pp. 213–244.

of order? Rather there has always been a multitude of traditions and of usually mutually exclusive principles of order.[62] The European Union, too, will not and cannot pretend to own and propagate the only one. But surely it has developed one and possibly the most relevant model of order for tomorrow's Europe. To consolidate and expand it, however, can succeed only if the Union's members want it and are prepared to provide the Union with the necessary authority and mechanisms to shape European politics accordingly. In other words: a new 'European architecture' would seem impossible without a 'new architecture' of the European Union.[63]

So much the aim. Reality is still different, more complex and more sobering. A common foreign and security policy of the Union is still a distant goal. It may even never be reached. Such recognition is painful for those who see in this goal a central precondition for preserving peace and stability on the continent. Still, such recognition can also be helpful. It can close the gap between expectation and reality, between promise and delivery. At the same time it can stimulate thinking, if not action, towards what a Union with its powerful potential can and should do in a world where the temptation of nationalism and separatism would still seem to be irresistible. Some steps towards a more effective and dynamic common foreign and security policy are possible.

Creating analytical capabilities

First, to take up a suggestion that has been in the air for a long time and is now repeated by the high-level group referred to above: the Union should create a central analysis and evaluation capability to assist the foreign policy making process. Such capability would allow one to detect central areas in which the Union and its institutions (Council and Commission in the first place) should act and define their priorities and objectives. Even if the Union cannot, for the foreseeable

---

62 J. R. von Salis, Die Wirklichkeit Europas, in: Europa – Weltmacht oder Kolonie? Hrsg. von G.-K. Kaltenbrunner, München 1978, p. 35.
63 Cf. H. Kramer, The European Community's Response to the 'New Eastern Europe', op. cit., p. 240.

future, develop its own defence capacity, the security and military dimensions must be included in such an analysis and introduced into foreign policy considerations. The creation of such an independent centre would not require a change of the Maastricht Treaty. It therefore depends exclusively on the will of the member states and the Council.

Reducing the scope of foreign policy

The second step is not institutional but conceptual in nature. Hence it is more delicate and surely more difficult to implement. We are arguing here for two interrelated concepts. First, in order to make common foreign policy more effective, its scope should be reduced.[64] In other words: the Union will have to concentrate its forces on those issues and regions which are not only important but where it can hope to achieve the best possible results. This may demand both courage and unity. To say 'no' is always more difficult than to say 'yes'. However, in the end it will increase both the credibility of what the Union can do, and its impact once it is done.

In terms of truly strategic commitments, the three peripheries – Russia and the CIS, South-East Europe and the Mediterranean – must remain at the very core of the Union's foreign and security policy. This does not exclude, of course, agreements on cooperation of various kinds with other regions, nor indeed reinforcing the transatlantic relationship. But a Union enlarged with countries from Central and Eastern Europe will increasingly depend, for its economic well-being, its political stability and its strategic security, on similar conditions in its immediate neighbourhood. It has therefore every interest to promote and consolidate such conditions as a priority goal. To stretch such or similar commitments much beyond risks weakening the intensity and credibility of the former while adding little if anything to strengthening the latter. It would

64 Cf. Reinhardt Rummel, EPZ – Erfolgsformel für die Gemeinsame Europäische Außenpolitik?, op. cit., and his article 'Integration, Disintegration, and Security in Europe – Preparing the Community for a Multi-Institutional Response, in: International Journal, Vol. XLVII (Winter 1991–1), pp. 64–92.

be a typical case of overstretch. The emerging dispute about the distribution of aid to the Lomé-Convention countries demonstrates what may become a recurrent theme within the Union in the future: the definition of priorities on the one hand, and the maintenance of an equilibrium in the distribution of scarcer means on the other. Such a struggle between conflicting aid commitments is likely to become fiercer as the Union will take in more, and mostly economically weak, countries – while wishing to expand its global activities at the same time.

Common foreign and security policy should ideally emanate from a Union that is sufficiently united. To arrive at the necessary consensus still requires a complex and often tortuous process of consultation and bargaining. Such process can have, if all goes well, a positive and eventually unifying effect. But it can also become divisive. It can lay open divergencies hitherto hidden or dormant and never spelled out. To agree on such intricate issues (as was the recognition of Croatia) is an exercise of high diplomacy with often low returns.

Building and accepting a consensus on foreign policy issues is therefore a process that is as difficult as it is delicate. It is even more difficult as long as the Union cannot, often for understandable reasons, agree on a simplified and efficient structure of foreign policy making. The Treaty of Maastricht has, to be sure, created a more institutionalized structure to that effect. But it is still very cumbersome and not particularly effective. It reveals that member states are, for better or worse, still very reluctant to delegate foreign and security matters to the higher, European level. The present institutional set-up is therefore a soft compromise between the European Commission, the Council and the member states, the latter retaining the last word whenever and wherever unanimity is required. The best we can therefore expect for the foreseeable future and, most likely, beyond the Intergovernmental Conference scheduled for 1996, are small steps, a rapprochement on this or that issue, consensus on specific but most marginal issues, and occasional common actions that follow from it.

If such an analysis and forecast is not too far from reality, would it not be better and, in fact, more honest, to renounce sweeping foreign policy and security goals for which a consensus is unlikely or, at best, attainable only on the smallest common denominator? On the other hand, it could be useful and would surely be more realistic, to define those fields of action on which all, or most, of the member states are likely to agree and join forces when they have to be translated into concrete action.

Such a proposal comes close to the idea that, thanks to the very dynamics of international politics, the Union is propelled to do things, or accept responsibilities, for which it was originally neither competent nor equipped. Nobody would have predicted, in 1989, that a year later it was called upon to take a stand against a country (Iraq) with which many of its members entertained close commercial and political relations. No less unexpected was the Union's participation in sanctions against Serbia. Both actions went beyond what one would have expected from a civil power. Almost imperceptibly, *par la force des choses*, the Union is assuming tasks that seemed to belong to the untouchable sphere of state sovreignty. They now, under rapidly changing circumstances and in face of new situations, are being delegated to the Union. Member states reluctantly come to the conclusion that their interests may be better expressed through collective action than if they do it on their own. 'Action by delegation'[65] might be the appropriate description for this process of gradual merger between national and common (European) interests.

Towards a 'sectoral neutrality'?

It is the experience of every confederate state to be particularly circumspect when it comes to handling foreign policy issues. The neutrality of Switzerland has as much to do with the concern to keep peace at home as with the interest to stay out of conflict abroad. An active foreign policy of the central government does not necessarily promote internal cohesion amongst the confederate states – be they cantons, Länder or republics. All have their own views and interests. They sometimes converge and sometimes diverge. But they always require the federal government to tread carefully and avoid extreme decisions.

65 Dominique David, La Communauté entre la paix et la guerre, op. cit., p. 90.

If it does not, it risks resistance on part of its member states to anything that looks like a national foreign policy which, for reasons of their own, they cannot identify with, let alone support.

The European Union finds itself today in a situation that bears some resemblance to that of confederations like that of the United States and Switzerland, particularly in the early years of their existence. Both had to try to reconcile the political interests and specificities, historic sensitivities or special relationships of their member states. George Washington's advice to his compatriots to beware of foreign 'entanglement' – meaning: with Europe – was a wise one; the decision to opt for neutrality its only logical conclusion. Switzerland, following an already long-standing practice, got her neutrality confirmed by the Congress of Vienna in 1815 and has, with occasional differentiations, observed it ever since. For both countries national cohesion of their then still fragile community was more important than a potentially divisive international activism.

Now it may be the European Union's turn. It may come to a similar conclusion inasmuch as a cautious abstinence on those issues might be advisable for which the price of a commitment abroad risks being too high compared with the frictions it may provoke within. To be sure, it will not be easy to foresee and to appraise on which issues and at what moment such tension will arise. But everybody is clearly aware of which issues are particularly prone to cause friction or may even be beyond minimal consensus. There are regions which, as pointed out before, are of higher priority than others; and there are issues on which action is more important than on others.

There are two ways to deal with the problem. One is what we call 'sectoral neutrality': its function would be to prevent the Union from getting stuck with secondary issues instead of addressing those which are really central to its mission while at the same time unnecessarily causing internal disputes on questions of only limited importance.[66] Nobody can force the Union in its present state of incomplete integra-

---

66 Cf. Curt Gasteyger, Europäische Außenpolitik zwischen Vorsatz und Wirklichkeit (forthcoming); Laurent Goetschel, Die außen- und sicherheitspolitische Dimension der EU: Folgen für die Schweiz, Cahiers de l'IDHEAP, No 132, Lausanne, July 1994, p. 18.

tion to take positions on international issues for which either consensus is out of reach or it is not equipped to deal with adequately. A decision to abstain or to remain neutral, be it limited in time or in substance, would make the Union's foreign policy more predictable. It would also protect it against unnecessary friction or wasteful energy spent on secondary issues.

Coalitions for action

The other way of invigorating the Union's foreign policy is the possibility of forming 'coalitions for action'. They would be limited in time and/or substance but based on a broadly formulated consensus acceptable to all member states.

There are good reasons for such coalitions and possibly also a greater need for them. As the number of members grows, so will almost inevitably also that of specific interests. Geographic expansion is likely to accentuate specific regional concerns. Germany, Austria and the three Scandinavian countries feel a special responsibility towards Central and Eastern Europe. On the other hand, France, Spain, Italy, Portugal and Greece are more likely to be concerned with developments in the Mediterranean. Either of the groups, be it as a whole or by consensus of only some of its members, may find common ground for action more easily than if all Union members have to be involved.

Coalitions may also emerge less along regional and more along substantive lines. The Gulf war has shown that of all members, Britain and France are best equipped to deal with 'out of area' contingencies. They may therefore take the lead when it comes to dealing with regions or issues in which other member states are reluctant to get involved. And yet, if the Union has to take a stand and make its interest felt, all members may welcome, even if tacitly, when countries like France or Britain are prepared to act on their and the Union's behalf.

Flexibility and adaptability must surely be the catchword for both approaches, sectoral neutrality here, coalition-for-action there. Both are feasible because they are pragmatic in nature and yet essential for the Union. In other words, its economic power has to be backed up by, and matched with, a political capacity to put this power to use – both for the Union itself and for those who want to gain from it. Ideally, the two methods could induce governments to simplify an overloaded decision-making process and delegate more clearly defined authority to the Commission. It would still leave the Council with the difficult but more circumscribed task of defining the general conditions within which either the sectoral neutrality or the coalitions-for-action would be implemented.

A policy of conditionality

The Union's economic power, already referred to several times, can be – and in fact is being – used for attaining political purposes. It may be viewed as a kind of 'indirect foreign policy' or 'foreign policy in disguise'. This may be the reason why it is quite effective. Most of the agreements of association and cooperation the Union concluded in recent years, or is negotiating presently, link economic assistance to the fulfillment of a specific set of political conditions. As mentioned before, the disappearance of the communist model as an alternative makes it easier for the Union to insist still more on this linkage. Countries wishing either to receive economic help or seek association with, if not admission to, the Union must demonstrate the credit worthiness and viability of their political system. This includes minimum standards of democracy, market economy and respect for human rights. In other words, it is an agenda for political reform, a precondition for closer cooperation and, as such, a basic constitutive element for the kind of environment in which the Union wishes to live and on which it depends.

Thus the strength and coherence of the Union lie in its determination to make the admission of new members contingent upon their meeting specific political criteria. Never has this conditionality been more important than in connection with its enlargement towards the East. Here some ten reform countries – from the Baltic states via Central Europe to Slovenia – are waiting for admission to the Union, well knowing that they have to live up to the rules of the club. These rules may be stiff and not easy to comply with. They may prolong the process of ad-

135

mission. But in the end, they oblige the candidates to economic reforms and political standards they otherwise might not seek. At the same time they help the Union to preserve the kind of homogeneity on which both its European specificity and its internal unity depends. Conditionality is therefore essential not only as a precondition for enlargement but also for Europe's future order at large.

Useful, if not indispensable as such indirect foreign policy by way of economic power is, it is only a complement to, not a substitute for, the more traditional kind of foreign and, of course, security policy. It is in these two fields where the hard core of external relations lies. It is the daily fare of politicians and diplomats, negotiators and security experts. The Union's citizens at home no less than the world at large expect the Union to express at least its views, if not to defend its interests, when it comes to such controversial issues like conflict resolution in former Yugoslavia, the peace process in the Middle East, Moscow's action in Chechnya and the control of the arms trade.

Some of these – and surely many other – issues have to be dealt with on a case-by-case basis. Most of them are, however, linked today to economics writ large. Sanctions against Yugoslavia have an obvious economic connotation as in fact has assistance to Russia and the limitation of weapons export. In other words: the link between economics and politics is getting ever stronger. We therefore argue in favour of the Union making still more use of its economic power when it comes to dealing with countries or addressing issues that require its attention. In many instances, the Union has the upper hand: economic strength and performance are already today, and will no doubt be even more so tomorrow, prime weapons in international relations. Both will find a world in which territorial size and military prowess have lost much of their glamour and weight. It is up to the Union to take advantage of this.

A fourfold strategy

In order to narrow the still glaring gap between its actual power and its occasional impotence, the Union should adopt a fourfold strategy. It should:

136

- add a new and forward-looking *finalité politique* to its traditional and successful mission by purposefully strengthening its role as the principal ordering force in Europe and the adjacent areas;
- make its foreign and security policy more effective by reducing its scope and focussing it on the 'feasible essentials', and, linked to that,
- opt, in the interest of preserving the greatest possible internal cohesion, either for a 'sectoral neutrality' on issues on which no consensus can be reached, or for allowing ad-hoc 'coalitions-for-action' where, with the tacit agreement of all, only some member states are ready and capable to act; finally, it should
- broaden the scope and direction of 'conditionality' by using still more purposefully the Union's unique economic potential for attaining political objectives of general importance.

All this is feasible without major reforms, let alone changes in the Maastricht Treaty. It remains to be seen whether the Intergovernmental Conference will go beyond this. Surely, better institutional arrangements, rationalization and simplification of the decision-making process are sorely needed. But they will follow, rather than precede, a clearer definition of what the European Union should and can do as an international actor in its own right. The problem thus does not lie in more mechanical modifications and administrative streamlining, however desirable and overdue. The real problem lies in the definition of the Union's future mission and the way by which it actually can fulfill it.

The proposals made above may help – to an extent. But they cannot relieve the member states of their duty to state clearly and loudly what kind of common foreign and security policy they wish the Union to conduct on their behalf. As mentioned before: there is no such common policy 'without tears', without some delegation of authority and some reduction of sovereignty in favour of the whole. Few still believe in a politically fully united federal state. However, between such a federation and a loose association of like-minded but independent states remains a wide range of intermediate solutions. It may be inevitable to look for intermediary solutions that correspond better to the specific characteristics of Europe than the still often diverging interests of its states.

There is, however, a serious risk with such pragmatism. It is that the objective of integration, upheld for so many years, is gradually being diluted. We may therefore end up with a Europe of 'variable geometry', moving at various speeds, separated by different classes – from 'core members' to associates and 'friends of the Union' and eventually heading for new divisions and imbalances. This is hardly what will make Europe stronger and fitter to meet the many very demanding challenges of an uncertain future. It stands no longer for a mission but for resignation. It will inexorably move the Union away from the promise of constructive power to the fallacy of destructive impotence. Nothing worse could then happen to the Union than to be obliged to give a reply similar to the one which Adolf Thiers, the French statesman got when, in 1871, he appealed to Europe's major powers for help. He asked them for their intervention against emerging German hegemony, threatening the peace of Europe. The reply he got by one of the foreign ministers was then as telling as it might be today: "Je ne vois pas d'Europe" – I do not see any Europe.

This surely can and should not be the answer. Europe has long ceased to be merely a geographical notion or a mythical vision. It is no longer a battlefield for internecine wars or a springboard for imperial ambitions. The European Union itself is a political reality with its own integrated institutions. As such it can no longer take refuge behind claims of non-existence and hence non-responsibility. It is present and has, for both its members and the outside world, a mission. All now depends on whether, when called upon to fulfill the mission, it will be ready and able to do so.

Tables:

Table 1: Today's Europe

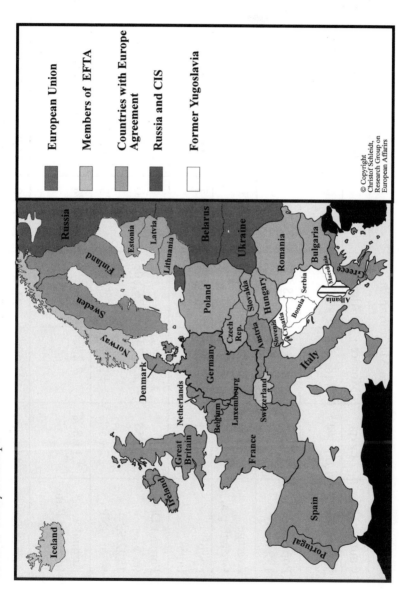

European Union

Members of EFTA

Countries with Europe Agreement

Russia and CIS

Former Yugoslavia

© Copyright
Christof Schleidt,
Research Group on
European Affairs

139

Table II: The Southern and Eastern Mediterranean

Country	Egypt	Morocco	Algeria	Libya	Tunisia	Syria	Turkey
Surface km²	1,001,449	446,550	2,381,741	1,759,540	163,610	185,180	779,452
Population 1994 (m)	60.7	27	28	5	8.7	14.3	60
Average Growth p.a.	2.4%	2.6%	3%	4.1%	2.3%	1.8%	5.4%
GNP (m $)	31,381	23,788	51,585	23,333	11,592	23,700	104,000
Foreign Debt (m $) 1992/93	39,855	23,524	26,806	2,100	7,534	16,900	59,400
% of GNP	126.5%	97.1%	53%	9%	62.6%	71.3	56.7%
Annual Inflation Rate 1992/93	11.8%	7.2%	6.6%	0.2%	7.4%	11.8%	61.9%
Armed forces	440,000	195,000	121,000	70,000	35,000	408,000	503,000

Sources: IISS, Military Balance 1994–95; Das Parlament, No. 43–44 (28.10.–4.11.1994), p.2; The Economist, Pocket World in Figures, 1994

Table III: Organizations for Europe

O
S
C
E

EFTA
• Switzer-land
• Liechten-stein

EU

• Finland*
• Sweden*

Nordic Council
• Norway
• Iceland
• Denmark

East Sea Council

Baltic Council
• Estonia*
• Lithuania*
• Latvia*

• Poland*

• Czech Rep.*
• Slovakia*
• Hungary*
Visegrád-Group

NATO-Cooperation Council

CIS
Kazakhstan*
Kyrgyzstan*
Tajikistan*
Turkmenistan*
Uzbekistan*
Belarus*

• Russia*

Armenia*
Azerbaijan*
Georgia*
Moldova*
Ukraine*

• Germany
• Belgium
• France
• United Kingdom
• Italy
• Luxembourg
• Netherlands
• Portugal
• Spain
• Greece

W
E
U

• Turkey

• Ireland
• Austria*

EEA

USA
Canada

NATO

• Andorra

• Albania*
• Bulgaria*
• Romania*

Black Sea Cooperation

• Slovenia*
• Croatia
• Bosnia-Herzegovina
  as Observer: Macedonia

• Malta*
• Monaco
• San Marino
• Holy See
• Cyprus

• = Members of the Council of Europe
* = Participants to "Partnership for Peace"

© Erich Schmidt Verlag

141

Table IV: The European Union's External Activities (based on Budget 1995)

External Activities	Amount (in m ECU)	Percentage
Actions Defined by Geographical Zones		
– Central and Eastern Europe & Former Soviet Union	1,582.6	32.4
– Latin America and Asia	670.5	13.7
– Mediterranean Area	487.4	10.0
– Other non-EU Countries	52.0	1.1
Food and Humanitarian Assistance		
– Food Aid	591.9	12.1
– Humanitarian Assistance	256.0	5.2
General Cooperation Activities		
– External Activities of Certain Communitarian Policies	294.2	6.0
– Other Cooperation Activities	646.8	13.2
– Common Foreign and Security Policy	110.0	2.3
– Overall Reserve for External Relations	190.0	4.0
	4,881.4	100

Table V: Distribution of Estimated Yearly Profits in the Year 2002 Following the Uruguay-Round

Billions US $

EU

China

Japan

USA

EFTA

Latin America

Rest of Asia

Table VI: The European Union's Network of Relations

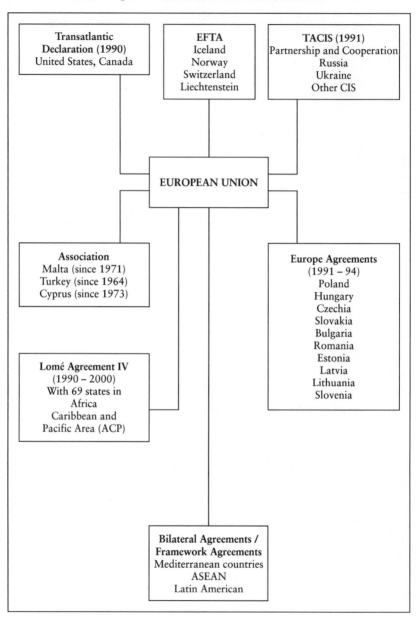

| Transatlantic Declaration (1990) United States, Canada | EFTA Iceland Norway Switzerland Liechtenstein | TACIS (1991) Partnership and Cooperation Russia Ukraine Other CIS |

EUROPEAN UNION

Association
Malta (since 1971)
Turkey (since 1964)
Cyprus (since 1973)

Europe Agreements
(1991 – 94)
Poland
Hungary
Czechia
Slovakia
Bulgaria
Romania
Estonia
Latvia
Lithuania
Slovenia

Lomé Agreement IV
(1990 – 2000)
With 69 states in
Africa
Caribbean and
Pacific Area (ACP)

**Bilateral Agreements /
Framework Agreements**
Mediterranean countries
ASEAN
Latin American

Table VIIa: European Commission: Total Cooperation with Latin America by Subregion, 1976–1993 (commitments, values in million of ECUs)

	1976–93	1976–80	1981–85	1986–90	1991–93	1991	1992	1993
Central America	1 079.53	40.26	211.55	459.93	367.79	106.21	125.07	136.51
Andean Group	901.73	33.66	148.55	378.89	340.63	84.57	121.40	134.66
MERCOSUR	248.44	3.25	17.42	69.84	157.93	39.42	49.93	68.58
Other LA Countries[1]	286.60	3.09	40.47	105.27	137.77	37.49	46.63	53.65
LA Regional[2]	171.55	12.36	17.08	48.69	93.42	31.09	31.29	31.04
Total	2 690.84	92.61	435.07	1062.63	1 100.53	300.80	374.32	425.41

1 Refers to Chile, Cuba and Mexico.
2 Programmes that cover the region as a whole. Sub-regional programmes are included in the totals for each group of countries.

Source: Institute for European-Latin American Relations (IRELA), Madrid, Dossier No. 51, December 1994: European Cooperation with Latin America in the 1990s: A Relationship in Transition (table established on the information from the European Commission)

Table VII b: European Commission: Humanitarian Aid Flows to Latin America by Subregion[1], 1976–1993 (commitments, values in million of ECUs)

	1976–93	1976–80	1981–85	1986–90	1991–93	1991	1992	1993
Central America	406.84	14.89	98.07	175.69	118.19	31.22	42.43	44.54
Andean Group	347.70	9.98	61.59	153.59	122.54	39.84	40.73	41.97
MERCOSUR	115.28	3.25	14.36	43.57	54.10	18.80	17.42	17.88
Other LA Countries[1]	193.41	3.09	38.59	79.01	72.72	24.60	19.62	28.50
LA Regional	3.16	–	–	1.18	1.98	0.45	1.37	0.16
Total	1 065.84	31.21	212.59	453.05	368.99	114.91	120.57	133.50

1   See notes for table VIIa.

Source: see table VIIa

Table VIII: The European Union as a Global Actor

	EUROPEAN UNION (15)	UNITED STATES	JAPAN
Area (1 000 km²)	3 337	9 373	378
Population (m)	368.7	258.3	124.7
Gross Domestic Product 1993 (1 000 m PPS*)	5 805.0	6 052.3	2 430.8
Per Capita Gross Domestic Product PPS*	15 733	23 430	19 500
Share World Trade 1993 in %** Exports Imports	20 19.2	16.3 20.4	8.2 12.7
Armed Forces 1994	2 080 150	Active: 1 650 500 Reserves: 2 048 000	237 700
Defence Expenditure 1994 bn $ /estimated	144.6	280	42.1

*   PPS = Purchasing power standard: a common unit representing an identical volume of goods and services for each country
** without Austria, Finland and Sweden
Sources: The European Union and World Trade, European Commission, Brussels, June 1995; International Institute for Strategic Studies, The Military Balance 1994–95, London, 1994

Table IX: How CFSP Works

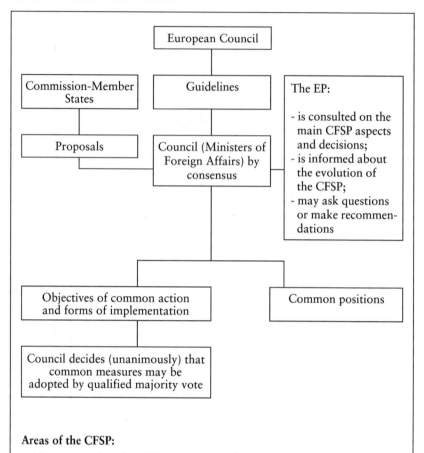

Areas of the CFSP:

- All matters related to EU security, including the possibility of developing a common defence policy.
- Joint action in areas where the member states have important interests in common.
- Joint action and the development of common positions in international conferences and organizations.

Source: Institute for European-Latin American Relations (IRELA), Madrid. Dossier No. 53: *The New Europe and Its Impact on Latin America,* p. 54 (table established on the information from the European Commission).

Table X: Joint Actions Adopted by the European Union on the Basis of Article J.3 of the Treaty on European Union

1. **Former Yugoslavia**	8 Nov. 1993	Support for the convoying of humanitarian aid in Bosnia-Herzegovina
	20 Dec. 1993	Supplementary
	7 March 1994	Extending the application of the 8.11.1993 Decision
	16 May 1994	Adapting and extending the application of the 8.11.1993 Decision
	27 July 1994	Supplementary
	12 Dec. 1994	Extending the application of the 8.11.1993 Decision
	12 Dec. 1994	Continued support for EU administration of Mostar
	6 Feb. 1995	Supplement (Mostar)
2. **Russian Parliamentary Elections**	9 Nov. 1993	Dispatch of a team of observers
3. **South Africa**	6 Dec. 1993	Support for the transition towards a democratic and multiracial South Africa
4. **Stability Pact**	20 Dec. 1993 14 June 1994	Inaugural conference Continuation
5. **Anti-personnel mines**	12 May 1995	Limitation on production, distribution, etc.
6. **Middle East peace process**	19 April 1994	Support for the peace process
7. **Non-proliferation of nuclear weapons**	25 July 1994	Preparation for the 1995 conference on the Non-proliferation Treaty
8. **Dual-use goods**	19 Dec. 1994	Control of exports of dual-use goods

Source: European Commission. Intergovernmental Conference 1995. Commission Report for the Reflection Group. Brussels, May 1995, p. 100

Abbreviations

ASEAN	Association of South-East Asian Nations
APEC	Asia-Pacific Economic Cooperation
CIS	Commonwealth of Independent States
CFSP	Common Foreign and Security Policy
CSCE	Conference on Security and Cooperation in Europe
EFTA	European Free Trade Association
EPC	European Political Cooperation
EU	European Union
GATT	General Agreement on Tariffs and Trade
NAFTA	North American Free Trade Agreement
NATO	North Atlantic Treaty Organization
NPT	Nuclear Non-Proliferation Treaty
WEU	Western European Union
OECD	Organization for Economic Cooperation and Development
OPEC	Organization of Petroleum Exporting Countries
OSCE	Organization for Security and Cooperation in Europe
WTO	World Trade Organization

The Author

Curt Gasteyger, Professor for International Relations at the Graduate Institute of International Studies in Geneva from 1974 until 1994 is now Honorary Professor and since 1978 Director of the Programme for Strategic and International Security Studies at the above Institute. He has been a member of the Steering Committee for the Project 'Strategies for Europe' sponsored by the Bertelsmann Foundation since 1987, and a member of the Advisory Board on Disarmament Matters at the United Nations in New York since 1993. He was Director of Programmes at the International Institute for Strategic Studies in London from 1964 to 1968 and Deputy Director of the Atlantic Institute for International Affairs in Paris from 1968 to 1974.

The Project Partners

Bertelsmann Science Foundation

In line with the aims and objectives set out in its statute, the Bertelsmann Science Foundation sees itself as an institution focussing on, inter alia, improving European and global cooperation and integration, and the competent organization of international cooperation in the fields of security, economics, politics, the arts and ecology as its main centers of activity.

This is also the approach it has taken since July 1995 to continue the "Strategies for Europe" project originally initiated by the Bertelsmann Foundation. By providing concepts and substance, the project is to contribute to the solution of present as well as future European policy problems. At the same time it is to improve communication between the countries of Europe and deepen European integration, while maintaining national and regional cultural identity. In order to provide conceptual support for this scheme, the Bertelsmann Science Foundation has set up an international strategy group, which consists of high-ranking experts from the fields of politics, economics and science. Results will be published, e.g. via the "Strategies for Europe" publication series.

The Research Group on European Affairs at the Geschwister-Scholl-Institute for Political Science affiliated to the Ludwig-Maximilians-University in Munich, is responsible for providing scientific assistance in developing and implementing the project objectives and the transfer of information. The Research Group is well suited for this task, as it can look back on many years of wide-ranging experience in intensive research into European questions. This work is documented in numerous publications on European unity and contributions to the "Jahrbuch der Europäischen Integration". In addition, the Research Group has comprehensive research facilities at its disposal. Apart from two editorial teams, these include a research library and the European Document Center, which has access to all documents and publications issued by the executive bodies of the European Union and is linked to the European data network.

The Publications

As a direct outcome of the work on the project "Strategies for Europe" the publications listed below have so far been issued:

Information on the approach, the objectives, the fields of work:

Bertelsmann Stiftung (ed.), *Strategien und Optionen für die Zukunft Europas. Ziele und Konturen eines Projektes.* Gütersloh 1988. 24 p. Free of charge.

Bertelsmann Foundation (ed.), *Strategies and Options for the Future of Europe. Aims and Contours of a Project.* Gütersloh 1989. 24 p. Free of charge.

Fondation Bertelsmann (ed.), *Stratégies et options pour l'avenir de l'Europe. Objectifs et countours d'un projet.* Gütersloh 1989. 24 p. Free of charge.

Fondazione Bertelsmann (ed.), *Strategie e opzioni per il futuro dell' Europa. Obiettivi e contorni di un progetto.* Gütersloh 1988. 22 p. Free of charge.

Bertelsmann Stiftung, *Ziele und Voraussetzungen eines geeinten Europas.* Vorstellung des Projektes "Strategien und Optionen für die Zukunft Europas". Mit Beiträgen von Valentin M. Falin, Henry A. Kissinger, Reinhard Mohn, Werner Weidenfeld. Gütersloh 1988. 44 p. Free of charge.

Werner Weidenfeld, Hermann Lübbe, Werner Maihofer, Joseph Rovan, *Europäische Kultur: das Zukunftsgut des Kontinents.*

154

Vorschläge für eine europäische Kulturpolitik. Gütersloh 1990. 124 p. Free of charge.

Werner Weidenfeld et al., *Herausforderung Mittelmeer – die europäische Antwort. Aufgaben, Ziele und Instrumente einer europäischen Politik.* Gütersloh 1991. 40 p. Free of charge.

In the series "Basic Findings":

Forschungsgruppe Europa, *Europäische Defizite, europäische Perspektiven – eine Bestandsaufnahme für morgen.* Grundlagen 1. Gütersloh 1988. 222 p., ISBN 3–89204–011–7. DM 20.00.

Research Group on European Affairs, *European Deficits, European Perspectives – Taking Stock for Tomorrow.* Basic Findings 1. Gütersloh 1989. 232 p., ISBN 3–89204–018–4. DM 20.00.

Rolf H. Hasse, *The European Central Bank: Perspectives for a Future Development of the European Monetary System.* Basic Findings 2. Gütersloh 1990. 280 p., ISBN 3–89204–036–2. DM 20.00.

Wolfgang Däubler, *Sozialstaat EG? Die andere Dimension des Binnenmarktes.* Grundlagen 3. Gütersloh 1989. 208 p., ISBN 3–89204–026–5. DM 20.00.

Wolfgang Däubler, *Market and Social Justice in the EC – the Other Dimension of the Internal Market.* Basic Findings 3. Gütersloh 1991. 216 p., ISBN 3–89204–041–9. DM 20.00.

Dieter Biehl, Horst Winter, *Europa finanzieren – ein föderalistisches Modell.* Grundlagen 4. Gütersloh 1990. 176 p., ISBN 3–89204–028–1. DM 20.00.

Bertelsmann Stiftung (ed.), *Die Zukunft Europas – Kultur und Verfassung des Kontinents.* Grundlagen 5. Gütersloh 1991. 334 p., ISBN 3–89204–048–6. DM 20.00.

Lutz Wicke, Burkhard Huckestein, *Umwelt Europa – der Ausbau zur ökologischen Marktwirtschaft.* Grundlagen 6. Gütersloh 1991. 256 p., ISBN 3–89204–049–4. DM 20.00.

Werner Weidenfeld, Josef Janning (eds.), *Global Responsibilities: Europe in Tomorrow's World.* Basic Findings 7. Gütersloh 1991. 2nd edition 1993. 240 p., ISBN 3–89204–053–2. DM 20.00.

Kenneth Button, *Europäische Verkehrspolitik – Wege in die Zukunft.* Grundlagen 8. Gütersloh 1992. 192 p., ISBN 3–89204–055–9. DM 20.00.

Kenneth Button, *Transport Policy – Ways into Europe's Future.* Basic Findings 8. Gütersloh 1994. 228 p., ISBN 3–89204–065–6. DM 20.00.

Klaus W. Grewlich, *Europa im globalen Technologiewettlauf: Der Weltmarkt wird zum Binnenmarkt.* Grundlagen 9. Gütersloh 1992. 352 p., ISBN 3–89204–054–0. DM 20.00.

Reinhard Rupprecht, Markus Hellenthal, *Innere Sicherheit im Europäischen Binnenmarkt.* Grundlagen 10. Gütersloh 1992. 392 p., ISBN 3–89204–058–3. DM 20.00.

Reinhard Rupprecht, Markus Hellenthal, Werner Weidenfeld, *Internal Security and the Single Market.* Gütersloh 1994. 62 p., ISBN 3–89204–140–7. DM 12.00.

Werner Weidenfeld (ed.), *Herausforderung Mittelmeer: Aufgaben, Ziele und Strategien europäischer Politik.* Grundlagen 11. Gütersloh 1992. 244 p., ISBN 3–89204–063-X. DM 20.00.

In the series "Working Papers":

Forschungsgruppe Europa (ed.), *Binnenmarkt '92: Perspektiven aus deutscher Sicht.* Arbeitspapiere 1. Gütersloh 1988. 4th edition 1989. 224 p., ISBN 3–89204–015-X. DM 12.00.

Werner Weidenfeld, Walther Stützle, Curt Gasteyger, Josef Janning, *Die Architektur europäischer Sicherheit: Probleme, Kriterien, Perspektiven.* Arbeitspapiere 2. Gütersloh 1989. 74 p., ISBN 3–89204–020–6. DM 12.00.

Bertelsmann Stiftung (ed.), *Die Vollendung des Europäischen Währungssystems.* Arbeitspapiere 3. Gütersloh 1989. 72 p., ISBN 3–89204–024–9. DM 12.00.

Werner Weidenfeld, Josef Janning, *Der Umbruch Europas: die Zukunft des Kontinents.* Arbeitspapiere 4. Gütersloh 1990. 72 p., ISBN 3–89204–032-X. DM 12.00.

Werner Weidenfeld, Christine Holeschovsky, Elmar Brok, Fritz Franzmeier, Dieter Schumacher, Jürgen Klose, *Die doppelte Integration: Europa und das größere Deutschland.* Arbeitspapiere 6. Gütersloh 1991. 108 p., ISBN 3–89204–042–7. DM 12.00.

Werner Weidenfeld, *Wie Europa verfaßt sein soll. Materialien zur Politischen Union.* Arbeitspapiere 7. Gütersloh 1991. 456 p., ISBN 3–89204–045–1. DM 12.00.

Werner Weidenfeld (ed.), *Der vollendete Binnenmarkt – eine Herausforderung für die Europäische Gemeinschaft.* Arbeitspapiere 11. Gütersloh 1993. 152 p., ISBN 3–89204–072–9. DM 12.00.

Further Publications:

Werner Weidenfeld (ed.), *Demokratie und Marktwirtschaft in Osteuropa.* Revised and updated version. Gütersloh 1995. 584 p., ISBN 3–89204–166–0. DM 48.00.

Werner Weidenfeld, Josef Janning (eds.), *Europe in Global Change.* Gütersloh 1993. 288 p., ISBN 3–89204–084–2. DM 34.00. 2nd edition.

Sergei A. Karaganov, *Whither Western Aid to Russia. A Russian View of Western Support.* Gütersloh 1994. 92 p., ISBN 3–89204–132–6. DM 15.00.

Grigorij Jawlinskij, *Reform von unten – Die neue Zukunft Rußlands.* Gütersloh 1994. 192 p., ISBN 3–89204–119–9. DM 25.00.

Werner Weidenfeld (ed.), *Das europäische Einwanderungskonzept.* Gütersloh 1994. 200 p., ISBN 3–89204–088–5. DM 25.00.

Werner Weidenfeld (ed.), *Maastricht in der Analyse. Materialien zur Europäischen Union.* Gütersloh 1994. 502 p., ISBN 3–89204–111–3. DM 25.00.

Werner Weidenfeld (ed.), *Europa '96. Reforming the European Union.* Gütersloh 1994. 60 p., ISBN 3–89204–154–7. Also in German ISBN 3–89204–151–2 (DM 10.00), French ISBN 3–89204–155–5, and Italian ISBN 3–89204–170–9. Free of charge. Spanish version out of print.

Peter Hardi, *Environmental Protection in East-Central Europe: A Market-Oriented Approach.* Gütersloh 1994. 136 p., ISBN 3–89204–137–7. DM 15.00.

Bertelsmann Foundation (ed.), *Central and Eastern Europe and the European Union. Problems and Prospects of Integration.* Gütersloh 1995. 172 p., ISBN 3–89204–164–4. Also in German. ISBN 3–89204–163–6. Free of charge.

Werner Weidenfeld (ed.), *Reform der Europäischen Union.* Materialien zu Revision des Maastrichter Vertrages 1996. Gütersloh 1995. 426 p., ISBN 3–89204–127-X. DM 20.00.

William R. Smyser, *The Europe of Berlin. On a New Division of Labor Across the Atlantic.* Gütersloh 1995. 48 p., ISBN 3–89204–182–2. DM 15.00.

Werner Weidenfeld (ed.), *Europa und der Nahe Osten.* Gütersloh 1995. 60 p., ISBN 3–89204–204–7. Also in Arabic ISBN 3–89204–210–1. DM 12.00.

Werner Weidenfeld, Jürgen Turek (eds.), *Standort Europa. Handeln in der neuen Weltwirtschaft.* Gütersloh 1995. 230 p., ISBN 3–89204–177–6. DM 25.00.

Miles Kahler, Werner Link, *Europa und Amerika nach der Zeitenwende – die Wiederkehr der Geschichte.* Gütersloh 1995. 176 p., ISBN 3–89204–148–2. DM 20.00.

Joseph Rovan, *Europa und die Welt von morgen.* Gütersloh 1995. 52 p., ISBN 3–89204–178–4. DM 15.00.

Hans-Holger Herrnfeld, *European by Law. Legal reform and the approximation of law in the Visegrad countries.* Gütersloh 1995. 182 p., ISBN 3–89204–806–1. Also in German. ISBN 3–89204–212–8. DM 25.00.

Werner Weidenfeld (ed.), *Central and Eastern Europe on the Way into the European Union. Problems and Prospects of Integration 1995.* Gütersloh 1995. 270 p., ISBN 3–89204–216–0. Also in German. ISBN 3–89204–214–4. DM 10.00.

Bertelsmann Foundation (ed.), *Europe's Political Agenda for the Nineties.* International Bertelsmann Forum. Gütersloh 1995. 174 p., ISBN 3–89204–136–9. Also in German. ISBN 3–89204–135–0. DM 20.00.

Wolfgang H. Reinicke, *Deepening in Atlantic. Toward a New Transatlantic Marketplace?* Gütersloh 1996. 96 p., ISBN 3–89204–802–9. DM 18.00.

Curt Gasteyger, *An Ambiguous Power. The European Union in a Changing World*. Gütersloh 1996. 160 p., ISBN 3–89204–807–X. DM 20.00.

Heinz Laufer, Thomas Fischer, *Föderalismus als Strukturprinzip für die Europäische Union*. Gütersloh 1996. 196 p., ISBN 3–89204–801–0. DM 20.00.

Wolfgang Reinicke, *Tugging at the Sleeves of Politicians. Think Tanks – American Experiences and German Perspectives*. Gütersloh 1996. 72 p., ISBN 3–89204–236–5. Also in German. ISBN 3–89204–235–7. DM 12.00.

Georg Brunner, *Nationality Problems and Minority Conflicts in Eastern Europe*. Updated and completely revised edition. Gütersloh 1996. 198 p., ISBN 3–89204–808–8. Also in German. ISBN 3–89204–800–2. DM 25.00.

Werner Weidenfeld, *America and Europe: Is the Break Inevitable?. Gütersloh 1996. 148 p., ISBN 3–89204–249–7. Also in German. ISBN 3–89204–228–4. DM 32.00.*

Franco Algieri, Josef Janning, Dirk Rumberg (eds.), *Managing Security in Europe. The European Union and the challenge of enlargement*. Gütersloh 1996. 272 p., ISBN 3–89204–805–3. DM 30.00.

Josef Janning, Dirk Rumberg (eds.), *Peace and Stability in the Middle East and North Africa*. Gütersloh 1996. 142 p., ISBN 3–89204–243–8. DM 20.00.

Werner Weidenfeld (ed.), *Entral and Eastern Europe on the Way into the European Union*. Problems and Prospects of Integration in 1996. Gütersloh 1996. 280 p., ISBN 3–89204–812–6. DM 15.00.

Werner Weidenfeld (ed.), *Neue Ostpolitik – Strategie für eine gesamteuropäische Entwicklung*. Gütersloh 1997. 192 p., ISBN 3–89204–810–X. Short Version: A New Ostpolitik – Strategies for a United Europe 32 S., ISBN 3–89204–815–0. Free of charge.

Stefan Collignon, *Geldwertstabilität in Europa*. Die Währungsunion auf dem Prüfstand. Gütersloh 1996. 200 p., ISBN 3–89204–811–8. DM 25.00.

Max Kaase, Andrew Kohut, *Estranged Friends? The Transatlantic Consequences of Societal Change*. Gütersloh 1996. 152 p., ISBN 3–89204–149–0. DM 15.00.

Werner Weidenfeld, Josef Janning, Sven Behrendt, *Transformation in the Middle East and North Africa*. Gütersloh 1997. 60 p., ISBN 3-89204-278-0. DM 15.00.

Wolfgang H. Reinicke, *Die Transatlantische Wirtschaftsgemeinschaft. Motor für eine neue Partnerschaft?*. Gütersloh 1997. 120 p., ISBN 3-89204-303-7. DM 18.00.